JAN 2 0 2005

W9-BNI-094

Ansel Adams

The People to Know Series

Ansel Adams
0-7660-1847-4

Madeleine Albright
0-7660-1143-7

Neil Armstrong
0-89490-828-6

Isaac Asimov
0-7660-1031-7

Robert Ballard
0-7660-1147-X

Margaret Bourke-White
0-7660-1534-3

Garth Brooks
0-7660-1672-2

Barbara Bush
0-89490-350-0

Willa Cather
0-89490-980-0

Bill Clinton
0-89490-437-X

Hillary Rodham Clinton
0-89490-583-X

Bill Cosby
0-89490-548-1

Walt Disney
0-89490-694-1

Bob Dole
0-89490-825-1

Marian Wright Edelman
0-89490-623-2

Bill Gates
0-89490-824-3

Ruth Bader Ginsberg
0-89490-621-6

John Glenn
0-7660-1532-7

Jane Goodall
0-89490-827-8

Al Gore
0-7660-1232-8

Tipper Gore
0-7660-1142-9

Billy Graham
0-7660-1533-5

Alex Haley
0-89490-573-2

Tom Hanks
0-7660-1436-3

Ernest Hemingway
0-89490-979-7

Ron Howard
0-89490-981-9

Steve Jobs
0-7660-1536-X

Helen Keller
0-7660-1530-0

John F. Kennedy
0-89490-693-3

Stephen King
0-7660-1233-6

John Lennon
0-89490-702-6

Maya Lin
0-89490-499-X

Charles Lindbergh
0-7660-1535-1

Jack London
0-7660-1144-5

Malcolm X
0-89490-435-3

Wilma Mankiller
0-89490-498-1

Branford Marsalis
0-89490-495-7

Anne McCaffrey
0-7660-1151-8

Barbara McClintock
0-89490-983-5

Rosie O'Donnell
0-7660-1148-8

Gary Paulsen
0-7660-1146-1

Christopher Reeve
0-7660-1149-6

Ann Richards
0-89490-497-3

Sally Ride
0-89490-829-4

Will Rogers
0-89490-695-X

Franklin D. Roosevelt
0-89490-696-8

Charles M. Schulz
0-7660-1846-6

Steven Spielberg
0-89490-697-6

John Steinbeck
0-7660-1150-X

Martha Stewart
0-89490-984-3

Amy Tan
0-89490-699-2

Alice Walker
0-89490-620-8

Andy Warhol
0-7660-1531-9

Elie Wiesel
0-89490-428-0

Simon Wiesenthal
0-89490-830-8

Frank Lloyd Wright
0-7660-1032-5

People to Know

Ansel Adams

American Artist with a Camera

Joel Strangis

Enslow Publishers, Inc.

40 Industrial Road   PO Box 38
Box 398   Aldershot
Berkeley Heights, NJ 07922   Hants GU12 6BP
USA   UK

http://www.enslow.com

For Diane, my wife and partner

Library of Congress Cataloging-in-Publication Data

Strangis, Joel.
    Ansel Adams : American artist with a camera / Joel Strangis.
        p. cm. — (People to know)
    Summary: Discusses the life and accomplishments of Ansel Adams, including the
care he took in the outdoors to ensure the best photographs, and the equal care he
took in the darkroom to obtain first-quality prints.
    Includes bibliographical references and index.
    ISBN 0-7660-1847-4
    1. Adams, Ansel, 1902—Juvenile literature. 2. Photographers—United States—
Biography—Juvenile literature. [1. Adams, Ansel, 1902–1984. 2. Photographers.]
I. Title. II. Series.
TR140.A3 S77 2002
770'.92—dc21

                       2002001187

Printed in the United States of America

10 9 8 7 6 5 4 3 2 1

To Our Readers:
We have done our best to make sure all Internet Addresses in this book were active and
appropriate when we went to press. However, the author and the publisher have no control over and assume no liability for the material available on those Internet sites or on
other Web sites they may link to. Any comments or suggestions can be sent by e-mail
to comments@enslow.com or to the address on the back cover.

Every effort has been made to locate all copyright holders of material used in this book.
If any errors or omissions have occurred, corrections will be made in future editions of
this book.

Illustration Credits: ©1981 Center for Creative Photography, Arizona Board
of Regents, p. 73; Archive Photos/Getty Images, pp. 33, 106; Courtesy of the
Bancroft Library, University of California, Berkeley (19xx.066:22–ACB; Muir,
John – POR 65; Adams, Ansel – POR 3), pp. 18, 24, 41; Courtesy of the
Gerald R. Ford Museum, p. 109; From the Roy D. Graves Collection,
Courtesy of the Bancroft Library, University of California, Berkeley
(1906.17500 v.8:40), p. 13; Library of Congress, pp. 53, 77, 79, 88; National
Archives, pp. 31, 45, 56, 68, 70, 76, 84, 100; Photograph by Cedric Wright.
Courtesy of Colby Memorial Library, Sierra Club, p. 9; Photograph by
Francis P. Farquhar. Courtesy of the Farquhar family. Reproduction print fur-
nished by the Collection Center for Creative Photography, The University of
Arizona, pp. 38, 49; Photograph by J. Malcolm Greany. Courtesy of the
Greany Family. Reproduction image furnished by the Bancroft Library,
University of California, Berkeley (Adams, Ansel – POR 4), p. 93; Property of
the author, p. 30.

Cover Illustration: Photograph by J. Malcolm Greany. Courtesy of the
Greany Family. Reproduction image furnished by the Bancroft Library,
University of California, Berkeley (Adams, Ansel – POR 4).

Contents

Acknowledgments

Many individuals assisted in the preparation of this work. First and foremost my wife, Diane Strangis, read the manuscript, made helpful comments, and kept me on course. Ted Hartwell, curator in the Department of Photography at the Minneapolis Institute of Arts, and his assistant, Caroline Wanstall, gave encouragement and guidance to my early efforts.

On behalf of their families, Peter Farquhar generously permitted the use of two photographs of Ansel Adams his father had taken during their excursions in the Sierras and Patrick Greany generously allowed the use of his father's photograph of Adams in Alaska. The staff in the Research Room of the Still Pictures Branch of the National Archives was very helpful to me during a Saturday morning visit.

There is a story for every photograph in this book, and I am especially grateful to Susan Snyder and Erica Nordmeier at the Bancroft Library, University of California at Berkeley; Leslie Calmes, Denise Gose, and Dianne Nilsen at the Center for Creative Photography, University of Arizona; Ellen Byrne at the Sierra Club; Rosa DiSalvo and Gary Bent at Getty Images; and Kenneth Hafeli at the Gerald R. Ford Museum. Also my thanks to the librarians and staff of the Fine Arts Library at the University of Florida and the Alachua County (Florida) Public Library.

A Photograph at Dawn

In the darkness of a cold morning in December 1943, Ansel Adams woke up early with the hope of making a sunrise photograph.[1] His wife, Virginia, rose, too, and prepared a thermos of coffee.

Ansel and Virginia Adams were in Manzanar, California, near the state's eastern border. That winter, America was in the middle of World War II. Too old to enlist in the armed forces, Adams had used his experience as an outdoorsman to escort troops on practice missions through the mountain regions of California. He had also used his skill as a photographer to teach soldiers the basics of military photography. But Adams believed in the importance of beauty, and he wanted to use his camera to capture images that would help Americans remember what they were fighting for.[2]

Leaving Manzanar, the couple drove fifteen miles south to the small town of Lone Pine and stopped at a spot that looked westward to Mount Whitney and the surrounding mountains, the Sierra Nevada. Adams wanted a dramatic photograph of Mount Whitney, the tallest mountain in the United States outside of Alaska.

Adams had made this trip four times already. Each time heavy clouds had kept him from attempting a photograph.[3] This time a clear night sky promised a bright sunrise.

Predawn passersby would have seen a strange sight that night as a bearded man climbed onto a wooden platform mounted on top of a Pontiac station wagon.[4] Once on the platform, Adams set up his tripod, and on top of that his eight-by-ten Ansco view camera.[5] (An eight-by-ten camera uses a negative eight inches by ten inches in size.)

With the camera ten feet above the ground, Adams could look over nearby shrubs and rocks and focus on the natural wonders in the distance. In the foreground was a pasture. Behind the pasture were low, dark hills. Behind the hills, Mount Whitney rose more than fourteen thousand feet against a background of snow-covered mountains.

Adams returned to the car and waited in the dark, drinking coffee with his wife. As the first rays hit the top of the mountain he climbed onto the platform again. His goal was to capture snow-white peaks rising above shadow-covered hills. Adams shivered

Adams often set up his camera on the roof of his car to get the best view for a photograph.

on top of the car and watched the sun light the mountaintop.[6] As the sun crept higher in the sky, its rays crawled down the mountainside.

But Adams's picture was threatened. A horse in the pasture was also facing Mount Whitney. If the horse did not move, the bottom of the photograph would show a pasture dominated by a horse's rear end. Not normally a man of prayer, Adams placed his hands together and looked heavenward.[7] Almost on cue, the horse turned sideways and Adams clicked the shutter. Moments later the sun flashed above the eastern horizon and the contrast between sunlit peaks and shadowed hills disappeared.

Adams's perfect image still had one problem. Youngsters from Lone Pine had outlined the initials "LP" with whitewashed rocks on one of the hills. When Adams developed the negative, the white "LP" was clearly visible. Adams was interested in capturing natural beauty, not the graffiti of teenagers. He covered the initials as best he could in the negative, and in the final print he spotted them over with ink. For his entire life, Adams was an outspoken advocate of "pure photography"—not tampering with a photograph to change what was there—but in this case he made an exception.

Winter Sunrise, the Sierra Nevada, from Lone Pine became one of Adams's most famous photographs. The dramatic contrast of shadowed hills and sunlit peaks, while preserving the details of the horse and the pasture in the foreground, captures the essence of black-and-white photography.

Adam's life had its share of unexpected turns. He grew up near the Pacific Ocean and for many years thought he would be a pianist. Instead, his fame and fortune would come from his love of the mountains and his talent with a camera. Focusing on the wilderness areas he cherished, Adams became an accomplished artist and one of the most successful photographers in the world.

The Early Years

Ansel Adams was born with California in his blood. His grandparents on both sides had traveled west as pioneers. His grandfather William Adams arrived in California in 1850 on the heels of the Gold Rush and prospered by selling supplies to miners. By the 1860s, William was a successful lumberman, owning lumber mills and a fleet of ships to haul building materials along the California coast. He and his wife, Cassandra, had five children. Their youngest, Charles Adams, born in 1868, would become Ansel's father.

Ansel's mother, Olive Bray, was born in Iowa in 1862. While Olive was still a baby, her parents headed for California by wagon train. Olive Bray and Charles Adams met in San Francisco. They were married in 1896. Their only child, Ansel Easton Adams, was born in their San Francisco apartment on February 20, 1902.

In 1903, the Adams family moved a few miles west to a new home near San Francisco's famous Golden Gate—a gap in California's coastline that provided the entrance to San Francisco harbor. Ansel's childhood home was surrounded by sand dunes and wild places, but the famous Golden Gate Bridge would not be built until 1937, when Ansel was well into his adult years.

Ansel's father, known as Carlie, commuted each day to his office in downtown San Francisco. Carlie was a reluctant businessman who loved nature and science. As a young man he wanted to be an astronomer, but instead he was called on to operate the family lumber business.

On April 18, 1906, Carlie was at a business meeting in Washington, D.C., while Ansel and his mother were home in San Francisco. On that day Ansel, his governess, his mother, and their cook woke to the horrible shaking of a major earthquake. Their beds crashed against the walls. Windows exploded, and the chimney toppled over. The family ran outside. Fortunately, other than the missing chimney and broken windows, their house remained in good condition.

Four-year-old Ansel played in the yard while the adults tried to salvage what they could. An aftershock rocked the yard again, throwing Ansel against a low wall and breaking his nose. In the midst of the emergency, the bump on the youngster's nose was not considered serious.

While Ansel's injury and the damage to his home were relatively minor, the Great San Francisco Earthquake of 1906 had destroyed the city. Gas lines were broken and the city was in flames. Brick buildings collapsed. More than five hundred people were killed.

On the East Coast, Ansel's father seized bits of information from telegrams filled with panic. He immediately headed west. By the time he arrived in San Francisco, the army had taken charge to maintain order. Carlie had to obtain a pass to reach his home. After walking five miles from the city center, he saw refugees camped in his neighborhood. But his house was still standing and his family was safe.

The Great San Francisco Earthquake of 1906 left much of the city in ruins.

The full damage to Ansel's face was not immediately apparent, and by the time the break was diagnosed, it would have taken surgery to fix it. A doctor told the family, "Fix it when he matures," but Adams often joked, "Of course I never did mature."[1] He never had the break repaired and the bump on his nose became a permanent part of his appearance.

As a youngster, Adams played along the dunes and tidelands that flanked the opening to San Francisco harbor. Insects, tadpoles, and seagulls were his companions. Rocky cliffs, beaches, and creek beds were his playroom.

Ansel was just as active in school. He later described himself as a "hyperactive brat."[2] He refused to memorize his lessons, he fought with a classmate, and he laughed at the teacher. He did not lack intelligence; he just had other things he would have rather been doing. In frustration, Ansel's father withdrew him from school at age twelve.

At home, Carlie Adams instructed his son in French and algebra. Ansel read literature on his own. When he began to experiment on the family piano, his parents enrolled him in piano lessons. Ansel's formal education never went beyond the eighth grade, but for the next thirty years—until he in turn became a teacher of others—he sought teachers and advisers who could give him the instruction he needed.

When Ansel was thirteen, his education was concentrated in two areas. He studied piano with a neighbor, and he expanded his world with a gift from his father—a year's pass to San Francisco's Panama-Pacific International Exposition.

The Panama-Pacific International Exposition celebrated the opening of the Panama Canal, but it also showed that San Francisco had recovered from the earthquake of 1906. The fair featured art, architecture, industry, music, and amusements. American states and foreign nations presented exhibits representing their history and culture.

Ansel visited the fair almost every day. At the Palace of Fine Arts, he viewed the works of modern European painters. Other pavilions featured new inventions. Ansel visited one exhibit so often that he was allowed to demonstrate a new adding machine featured there. In another hall he found a piano and demonstrated his talent as a musician.[3] Every day ended with fireworks.

Life at home, however, was not as joyful. Carlie Adams was not a skillful businessman, and bad luck made his situation worse. From 1897 to 1907 his company lost six mills and twenty-seven ships to fire and other disasters. Carlie tried to recover by investing in a process that converted sawdust into industrial alcohol, but his partners betrayed him and the business failed.

By 1912 the family could no longer afford to employ the cook, the maid, and Ansel's governess. Carlie tried working as a life insurance salesman. Olive's sister Mary, who had come to live with the family, joined Ansel's mother in criticizing Carlie. Beginning in 1917 Carlie made a reasonable income by managing an office building, but his family never forgave him for having presided over the collapse of their fortune.

Despite his setbacks, Carlie found joy in astronomy. With a small telescope, he and Ansel searched the sky together. The family had fallen on hard times, but Carlie found the money for Ansel's piano lessons, the exposition pass, and, later, a camera. Carlie Adams was determined to help Ansel follow his dreams.

In April 1916, Ansel's aunt Mary gave him a book entitled *In the Heart of The Sierras* by J. M. Hutchings. In the 1850s, Hutchings had been among the first men of European descent to enter the Yosemite Valley deep in the Sierra Nevada—the mountain range along California's eastern border. Hutchings was so taken by the beauty of the valley that he spent most of the rest of his life promoting it. Eventually he owned a hotel and other businesses there.

Hutchings's descriptions of fir trees two hundred feet tall, of granite cliffs rising three thousand feet, of waterfalls plunging a thousand feet, and of a lake so calm it reflected like a mirror captured the teenager's imagination. Ansel's parents had promised a family vacation for that summer, perhaps to Santa Cruz or Puget Sound. But Ansel insisted, "The promised vacation *must* be in this incredible place."[4]

Ansel and his parents left for what had become Yosemite National Park on the morning of June 1, 1916. Today the trip from San Francisco to Yosemite would barely take an afternoon by automobile along concrete freeways. In those days, the trip was a two-day adventure. The family traveled east and then south by train. After lunch they transferred to the Yosemite Valley Railroad to climb into the mountains. As they passed through the Sierra foothills, temperatures soared, eventually reaching one hundred degrees. The overdressed passengers perspired, but their excitement rose as the train skimmed the banks of the tumbling Merced River.

By evening the train reached the town of El Portal, where Ansel and his parents spent the night in a hotel. After breakfast the family loaded into an open bus for the climb to Yosemite Park. In the final ten miles from El Portal to Yosemite, they climbed two thousand feet over narrow roads with dizzying drop-offs. Some passengers closed their eyes, but Ansel loved the adventure.[5]

At last the bus rounded a corner. Before them lay the great Yosemite Valley. Ansel would never forget his first impression:

> *white water, azaleas, cool fir caverns, tall pines and stolid oaks, cliffs rising to undreamed-of heights, the poignant sounds and smells of the Sierra, . . . [an] experience so intense as to be almost painful.*[6]

The family lodged in a tent camp operated by Jennie and David Curry. The tents were a comfortable alternative to expensive hotels. Inside the large tent, beds and a washbasin stood on a wooden floor. Canvas sides could be rolled up to admit daytime breezes and rolled down to block cold night air.

A few days after they arrived in Yosemite, Ansel's parents presented him with his first camera, a Kodak Brownie. These simple cameras with preloaded rolls of film had revolutionized the world of photography. At last it was possible for an amateur to take photographs without using cumbersome equipment.

Fourteen-year-old Ansel was stunned by the beauty of Yosemite Valley. This photo was taken by George Fiske in the 1880s.

Ansel carried the camera on his daily explorations. One day he wanted to photograph the granite cliff known as Half Dome. Climbing on an old tree stump, he took aim. Just as he was about to snap the shutter, the stump crumbled and Ansel tumbled to the ground. A few days later he deposited his film at a store in Yosemite Village.

When Ansel retrieved his pictures, the developer asked about that photograph. The image was reasonably good, said the man, but its negative was upside down from those before and after it.

Ansel's father had to remain in San Francisco the next summer, but Ansel returned to Yosemite with his mother and his aunt Mary. Ansel was popular in camp, and the busy, enthusiastic teenager seemed to know everyone. One of the adults was a retired mining engineer named Francis Holman. Uncle Frank, as Ansel called him, spent his days exploring the mountains as well as gathering specimens of birds for the San Francisco Academy of Sciences.

In July 1917 Holman took Ansel on his first camping trip into the backcountry of the High Sierra. With a mule to carry their equipment, the two men hiked to Lake Merced, spending four nights on the trail.[7] Holman taught the youngster how to camp, cook, and hike in the wilderness. He also told Ansel about the Sierra Club, a group that would be vitally important in Ansel's adult life.

3

The Artist as a
Young Man

Sixteen-year-old Ansel returned
to Yosemite in the summer of 1918. That year, for the
first time, he traveled on his own, leaving his mother,
aunt, and father behind in San Francisco. He spent
the summer in camp with the Curry family and on the
trail with Frank Holman. He also filled many hours
taking photographs, but he was not pleased with his
results.

Back in San Francisco at the end of the summer,
Ansel wanted to know how to improve his photographs. A neighbor, Frank Dittman, ran a
photo-finishing lab in his basement. Ansel asked
Dittman for a job so that he could learn the secrets of
the photographic process. Ansel's tasks included
picking up rolls of exposed film at drugstores and

returning with the finished prints in a day or two. He was more interested, however, in his duties as a darkroom assistant, helping to develop negatives and print photographs. Dittman liked the youngster but teased him because he talked so much about Yosemite, naming him "Ansel Yosemite Adams."

The winter of 1918–1919 was a difficult one for the United States. American soldiers were fighting World War I in Europe, but the Spanish influenza that was sweeping across the country proved even deadlier than the war. Ansel contracted the disease early in 1919. Fortunately, he recovered after a few weeks.

Ansel read as he recuperated; one of the books was about a colony of people with a contagious skin disease called leprosy. Suddenly he was afraid of germs everywhere: germs that could bring the flu, germs that could bring leprosy.

In the spring, despite being weak in body and still worried about diseases, Ansel wanted to return to Yosemite. The doctors favored bed rest, but Ansel's father agreed that fresh air and moderate exercise would be good for him. By mid-June, Ansel was at the Curry camp, walking a little farther each day and preparing for extended hikes with Uncle Frank. By the end of summer Ansel's illnesses, both physical and mental, were gone. As it would for the rest of his life, Yosemite had given Ansel physical strength and refreshed his mind.

By about 1920, Ansel had progressed enough as a photographer to receive his first paid assignment. The task seemed simple. A neighbor who taught kindergarten offered Adams a small fee to photograph her class.

In those days, indoor photography was complicated. Flashbulbs and photographic lights were not available. An indoor photographer needing extra light placed a small amount of flash powder, usually magnesium, in a pan and held it aloft. Then he opened the camera shutter and, using a trigger below the pan, ignited the powder. The small explosion would create sufficient light to capture the desired image.

On the appointed day, Adams arrived at the school, organized his camera equipment, and prepared the flash powder. But he made a mistake, putting five times the recommended amount of powder in the pan. Then he raised the pan, made bird sounds to get the children's attention, opened the camera shutter, and fired the flash powder.

Boom! The powder exploded, filling the room with a loud noise and bright light. When Adams recovered from the shock, he found the children hiding under their desks and crying at the top of their lungs. The teacher opened a window and black smoke billowed out. The local fire company charged to the school with sirens wailing. Luckily, no serious damage was done. Adams completed the class portrait outside, where artificial light was not required.

Fortunately, the summer of 1920 held other, more useful experiences for Adams. During his visits to Yosemite National Park, Adams had learned that the Sierra Club maintained a lodge in the valley as its Yosemite headquarters. Each summer, the club hired a caretaker for the lodge. The job included living on-site and providing club members with information about the park. In the fall of 1919, Adams joined the Sierra Club and applied for the caretaker's job for the following summer.

The members of the Sierra Club were proud of their tradition as the unofficial guardians of Yosemite. Their first president, John Muir, had fallen in love with the Yosemite Valley twenty years before it became a national park.

Muir had arrived in the Yosemite Valley in 1868 and returned to it in the summer of 1869, working as a shepherd. He was disgusted by the damage done by herds of sheep devouring the grass, causing erosion and other problems. Nor did he approve of the fields of hay and wheat that had changed the natural beauty of the valley. While working in the valley, Muir wrote essays on the wonderful world around him. They were published in national journals. By 1889, Muir was urging that Yosemite Valley and surrounding areas be placed in trust of the national government. His cry was heard, and in 1890 Congress established Yosemite National Park.

In 1892, Muir and his friends established the Sierra Club "to explore, enjoy, and render accessible the mountain regions of the Pacific Coast" and to preserve the natural beauty of the Sierra Nevada.[1] The twenty-seven founding members elected Muir as president, a position he would hold until his death in 1914.

In 1900, club secretary William Colby proposed an annual outing, up to four weeks in length, to encourage members to go into the mountains and "to hear

John Muir, right, founder of the Sierra Club, stands with President Theodore Roosevelt on Glacier Point above Yosemite Valley in 1903. Both men believed in the importance of preserving forest and wilderness areas.

the trees speak for themselves."[2] About this time, the club also acquired a stone cottage to be used as its headquarters in the park. Members named it LeConte Memorial Lodge in honor of Joseph LeConte, one of the club's founders.

In the fall of 1919, Colby approved Adams's application for membership and hired him as caretaker of LeConte Memorial Lodge for the 1920 season. The job was perfect for Adams. Working in his beloved Yosemite, he came in contact with many hikers who also loved the valley. While he could not be away from his post long enough to fully participate in Sierra Club outings, he could occasionally get away to take photographs.

But months in the park meant Adams would be away from his most important occupation at the time—practicing piano. Adams had shown a talent for the piano and with hard work had built his skills toward a music career. By 1918, Adams had graduated to an advanced teacher who expected him to practice five hours a day.

Spending summers in the Sierra Nevada, Adams was unable to keep up his piano work. During his first summer at the lodge he went without a piano, but in his second summer as caretaker (1921), Adams discovered a piano at the home of Harry Best.

Best operated Best's Studio, a small store that carried paintings, books, and souvenirs for tourists. He and his daughter lived next to the store. Harry's wife had died the year before, and seventeen-year-old Virginia was her father's assistant and housekeeper.

The Bests welcomed Adams and encouraged him to play their old piano. Adams was delighted to have an opportunity to practice, but he found more than a piano at Best's Studio. He was intrigued by Virginia Best. Like Adams, Virginia hoped for a career in classical music, using her fine voice as her instrument. She also shared Adams's love for Yosemite and his feeling of disgust at the growing commercialization of the wilderness.[3]

The young couple fell in love and wrote each other many letters over the winter months. In her letters, Virginia encouraged Ansel to practice his piano and not spend too much time on his photography. In September 1923, Adams told Virginia that he was earning some money by giving piano lessons, but he was also earning money from his photography. Once he could earn a full income as a concert pianist, however, taking pictures would be just a hobby.[4]

In the same letter, Adams laid down a philosophy that would be a theme for his entire life. He declared that when he did sell photographs, he would sell only "work of the highest quality."[5] He planned to achieve this quality by printing only from his finest negatives, using the best materials available, and printing the photographs with utmost care. These standards would ultimately make Adams not only a great photographer, but also a master of the darkroom techniques required to print outstanding photographs.

4

A Short History of Photography

Early photography was more chemistry than artistry. The first photograph was made by Joseph Niepce in France in 1826. Using a mixture of bitumen (a form of asphalt) and oil of lavender spread on a metal plate, Niepce recorded the view from a window of his home. After eight hours of exposure, the light parts of the image (which had received more reflected sunlight) had hardened, while the dark parts (which had received less sunlight) could be washed away.

The image in Niepce's photograph was crude, and the eight-hour exposure time was not practical. He formed a partnership with Louis Jacques Daguerre to improve the process, but Niepce died in 1833 and never saw the fulfillment of his work.

Daguerre experimented with a variety of silver compounds and found a way to record a permanent image by exposing a chemically coated silver plate for forty minutes or less.[1] The chemicals in his process included nitric acid, iodine, mercury, and various salts. In 1839 he announced his discovery. The invention received little attention until the French government bought the rights and made the discovery available to the public. Photographs produced by Daguerre's technique were called daguerreotypes.

Daguerre's process quickly spread to the United States. In the fall of 1839, Samuel F. B. Morse, inventor of the telegraph, photographed his daughter in New York. In the summer of 1840, he photographed his Yale University classmates at their reunion.[2]

When improvements reduced the exposure time to less than a minute, the demand for daguerreotype portraits surged. Portrait studios lined the main street of every American city. Approximately 30 million daguerreotype images were made in the United States between 1839 and 1860.[3]

Despite their popularity, daguerreotypes were cumbersome. The sitter had to remain perfectly still for up to a minute. The fragile images had to be kept in airtight glass cases. Each image was an original and could not be duplicated except by making a photograph of the photograph.

An Englishman, Henry Talbot, also working in the 1830s, learned to make prints on transparent paper. His paper image, however, was reversed left to right, and the light areas of the subject were dark, while the dark areas were light. He had created a negative. His images were not as sharp as those of Daguerre, but with a negative he could make many "positive" prints from a single exposure.

In 1850, Frederick Archer introduced a technique that used a mixture of plant fibers, nitrates, alcohol, and ether spread over a glass plate. Before exposure, the plate was made light-sensitive by soaking in a solution of silver nitrate. Since the plate was still wet when exposed, the technique was known as the wet-plate process.

The wet plate could be used for negatives or for direct prints. Images were sometimes printed on thin but durable metal plates called ferrotypes or tintypes. These could be carried in a pocket or sent through the mail without harm.

In the mid-1800s, the carte de visite, a photograph mounted on a small card, became extremely popular. Using a wet-plate negative and a camera with up to a dozen lenses, a photographer could inexpensively make as many likenesses as the customer desired. These two-and-a-half-by-four-inch card portraits were given to friends and family.

Outside the studio, however, the wet process posed a problem. Once exposed, the plates had to be developed before they dried. Consequently, photographers had to take their darkrooms with them. When they were away from their studios, photographers often used a tent or a specially fitted horse-drawn wagon as a darkroom.

The U.S. Civil War (1861–1865) brought photography to new levels as photographers followed soldiers to battle. Because exposure times were still relatively

Z. P. McMILLEN,
PHOTOGRAPHER,
Over Wilder's Book Store,
NEWARK, OHIO.

N.B. The negative of this picture never destroyed.
DUPLICATES furnished at any
time.

Neg. No.

In the mid-1800s, trading and collecting small portraits, called cartes de visite, was a popular craze. Right: Photographers advertised their services on the backs of the cards.

long, photographers were unable to record soldiers in motion. Most Civil War photographs in the field show soldiers stiffly posed before a battle or document rows of dead soldiers afterward.

After the war, photographers were often a part of the survey parties sent by the United States government to map the western territories. One of the most active of these was Timothy O'Sullivan, who had been a military photographer during the Civil War. In 1871 Sullivan traveled up the Colorado River and into the

Grand Canyon. In 1873 he photographed the remains of Native American villages that are now part of the Canyon de Chelly National Monument in Arizona.

On other western surveys, William Henry Jackson took pictures in the Rocky Mountains. He photographed the Yellowstone area in 1871. A year later his dramatic images helped persuade Congress to designate Yellowstone as the first national park.

Still using the wet-plate process, these western photographers transported not only their cameras and fragile glass plates, but their chemicals and darkrooms

Black Canyon from Camp 8 Looking Above Colorado River *by Timothy O'Sullivan, 1871. Adams admired O'Sullivan's work and collected his photographs.*

as well. The heavy equipment was pulled in wagons, strapped to horseback, floated in boats, and hand carried up steep trails.

Dry-plate negatives were introduced around 1880, and photographers no longer had to have a nearby darkroom. They could buy a supply of pre-sensitized glass plates, expose them at the appropriate time, and develop them later in the studio. When Adams began taking serious photographs in the 1920s, he used dry-plate negatives.

The first company in the United States to make dry plates was owned by George Eastman. But it was a small camera that was his big contribution. At the end of 1888, the Eastman Dry Plate and Film Company of Rochester, New York, introduced its Kodak camera. The camera was the size of a ladies' shoe box, preloaded with a roll of continuous film that permitted up to one hundred exposures. It was easy to use: Simply point the camera, press the button, and wind the film for the next exposure.

The price of the camera included the cost of processing the film. After taking all the pictures, the customer would send the camera back to the company. A few days later, Eastman would develop the customer's film and return his or her prints. For a small additional fee, the company would load another roll of film and return the camera. No wonder the company adopted the slogan "You press the button, we do the rest."[4]

Suddenly anyone could be a photographer. Families no longer relied on studio photographers for a record of their loved ones. Even a child could

The Steerage *by Alfred Stieglitz, 1907. In his photo of a transatlantic crossing—the wealthier immigrants on deck, poor people below—Steiglitz saw artistry in the shapes. Note the white x of a man's suspenders below, the white oval of a straw hat above, and the diagonal lines of the stairs, the large pipe, and the catwalk. Steiglitz was a pioneer in transforming photography into an artform.*

photograph a birthday party or a day at the beach. In 1900 Kodak introduced a smaller camera, the Kodak Brownie, especially for use by children. The camera sold for a dollar; a roll of film was fifteen cents. A version of the Kodak Brownie was Adams's first camera on his trip to Yosemite.

The time from Daguerre's announcement in 1839 to Adams's first photograph in 1916 was seventy-seven years. Even though flashbulbs would not be invented until 1925 and film for color photographs would not be available until 1942, the science of photography had made great strides.[5] Photography had moved from a great experiment to a hobby a child could enjoy. When Adams started taking pictures, the challenge for serious photographers was not just to make an image, but to make an image of value.

"Let's Do a Portfolio"

While on a Sierra Club outing in the summer of 1923, Adams encountered Cedric Wright. Ansel and Cedric had met years before, when Cedric's father was Carlie Adams's attorney. Although Ansel was almost thirteen years younger than Cedric, the two men quickly became friends. Wright was a violinist and, like Adams, enjoyed hiking through the beautiful Yosemite Valley with his camera.

Wright's large redwood home in Berkeley, across the bay from San Francisco, was a gathering place for Sierra Club members. He was famous for re-creating trail dinners of spaghetti, bread, salad, cookies, and strong coffee. Adams was a frequent and popular visitor.

In April 1926 Wright asked Adams to bring some photographs to a party. At the gathering, Wright urged Albert Bender to look at Adams's photographs. Bender was a successful businessman with a reputation for helping artists. After a brief look, he invited Adams to bring the photographs to his office the next day.

In his San Francisco office, Bender carefully reviewed each of Adams's photographs. He asked a few questions, then said, "Let's do a portfolio."[1]

It was decided that Adams would make one hundred portfolios of eighteen handprinted photographs. Each collection would be placed in an attractive cover and sold for $50. Bender ordered ten sets and wrote Adams a check for $500. Then he telephoned his wealthy friends. By the end of the day, Bender had sold fifty-six sets.[2]

Bender also introduced Adams to other artists in the San Francisco area. At Bender's home, Adams met the photographer Edward Weston. Bender showed Weston some of Adams's work, but Weston was not impressed. He called the photographs "promising but immature." He was more taken with Adams's piano playing.[3]

It is not surprising that Weston was more interested in Adams as a musician than as a photographer. Adams still considered himself a pianist first and a photographer second. For Adams, photography was a sideline by which he could earn money to support his effort to become a professional musician.

As he passed his twenty-fifth birthday, Adams's concept of photography was unsophisticated. By his own admission, his early photographs were often no more than a "visual diary" of his mountain trips.[4] He recorded for others what he had seen, but he rarely tried to create art or convey feelings. That changed in the spring of 1927.

On a beautiful April day, Adams, Virginia Best, Cedric Wright, and two other friends decided to climb to an overlook of the Yosemite Valley called the Diving Board. Adams took along a large Korona view camera, twelve glass photographic plates, a wooden tripod, and some lens filters—more than forty pounds of equipment. The group climbed throughout the morning, stopping occasionally to take pictures. Despite the April sunshine, snow still painted the higher elevations.

The group reached the Diving Board at noon. From there they had a spectacular view of the valley and of Half Dome, a granite mass rising up thousands of feet from the valley floor. Adams wanted to photograph the craggy rock cliff that formed the face of Half Dome, but it was still covered by morning shadows. The group waited for sunshine to light the mountain.

Adams had used seven of his twelve photographic plates earlier in the day. While waiting for the shadows to clear, he took three more photographs.[5] As the sun's rays crept across the face of the cliff, Adams had only two plates left.

Shortly after two o'clock, Adams focused his camera on the rock wall, using a wide-angle lens. He covered the lens with a yellow filter to remove the haze, exposed the glass plate at the rear of camera, and released the shutter.

Adams was still not satisfied. It would be a fine picture, but it would not convey the emotions he felt.

In this 1927 portrait taken in the Sierra Nevada, Adams sports his favorite garb—knickers and sneakers.

Adams wanted a photograph that would capture the feeling of the "monumental shape . . . the brooding cliff with a dark sky."[6]

For the final exposure, Adams replaced the yellow filter with a red one that would create a dramatic contrast between sky, snow, and stone. He squeezed the shutter release, then packed up his equipment for the trip back down the mountain.

In the darkroom that night, Adams was pleased with his efforts. On the last plate, the powerful mountain seemed to rise up from a band of snow toward the sky—which he had changed from an innocent light blue to a dark void. He entitled the image *Monolith, The Face of Half Dome* and vowed to include it in his portfolio.

It was the first time Adams used a process he would later call *visualization*—or, as he defined it, "'seeing' the final print while viewing the subject."[7] In this process, *before pointing the camera*, the photographer visualizes the feelings he wants to project and the photograph that he will create. Once the photographer has a clear vision of what he wants to achieve, he decides where to place the camera, then chooses which lens, exposure setting, and darkroom techniques to use.

As Adams expanded his photography techniques, he was also making strides in other areas. The year 1927 was pivotal in many respects. Adams had his breakthrough as an artist with the photograph of Half Dome. He finished his portfolios for Bender, which gave him much-needed cash. He traveled to New Mexico with Bender, discovering new cultures and new landscapes. In July he went on his first full Sierra Club outing. Then, at the end of the year, he made a commitment to Virginia.

Adams's romance with Virginia Best had been on and off since they had met six years earlier. As early as 1923, the two had talked about marriage, but Adams cooled the relationship and started dating other women. In addition, rather than spend his summers in Yosemite near Virginia, Adams spent long portions of the summers of 1925 and 1926 on expeditions in the Sierra Nevada—neglecting Virginia, his music career, and his need to earn money. His camera, of course, never stayed behind.

On the day after Christmas, Adams showed up at the Best home in Yosemite with his friend Cedric Wright. Ansel proposed marriage and Virginia accepted. A week later, on January 2, 1928, the two were married at her home. Typically, Ansel wore knickers and sneakers.

Even marriage, however, could not keep Adams from mountain travel. William Colby invited him to be official photographer on the 1928 Sierra Club outing into the Canadian Rockies. Adams seldom missed the annual outing from then on. In 1930 he was appointed assistant manager of the trip.

In the three decades since Muir and Colby established the annual outing, it had grown immensely. Two hundred people traveled through pristine mountains for four weeks. One hundred mules carried their equipment. Adams's responsibilities included selecting each day's campsite, suggesting possible scenic climbs, and directing the campfire entertainment. He

*Albert Bender, center, shown here with Ansel and Virginia Adams,
liked to help young artists sell their work.*

made time for photography just after sunrise or just before sunset of each day.

Adams's duties to the group and his duties to his camera kept him busy. On one trip, at the end of the day Adams realized he had left a camera lens behind. Starting out after dark, he retraced his steps twelve miles back until he found the lens on a rock. He arrived back in camp at dawn, just in time to start that day's hike.[8]

Although often separated in the summer, Ansel and Virginia collaborated on an enjoyable winter project. In 1928 the owner of the largest hotel in Yosemite asked Ansel to entertain as a jester at the hotel's Christmas dinner. Adams climbed on log beams forty feet above the guests, who gasped and cheered. The next year Adams coproduced the pageant, renamed "Christmas Dinner at Bracebridge Hall." He directed the musicians, wrote the dialogue, and acted as host. Virginia sang a lead role. She and Ansel were important parts of the show until 1975.

Ansel Adams's life at the end of the 1920s resembled a poorly made photograph—his music, photography, marriage, Sierra Club trips, and Bracebridge dinners all blurred together without focus. It would take a trip to the ancient pueblos of New Mexico to help him choose one aspect of his life above all others.

The Making of a Photographer

On their 1927 trip to New Mexico, Albert Bender had introduced Ansel Adams to a colony of artists living near the town of Santa Fe. One of the artists was Mary Austin, a successful writer. Bender knew that Adams and Austin had similar views of nature, and he suggested they do a book together.

When Adams returned to Santa Fe with Virginia in 1929, Austin agreed to work with him on a book if they could find a suitable subject for her words and his photographs. To find a subject, they visited Austin's friend Mabel Dodge Luhan in Taos, seventy-five miles north of Santa Fe.

Originally from Buffalo, New York, Luhan had lived in Italy, Paris, and New York City. At each stop she had been the center of an artistic circle.[1] She was married to Antonio "Tony" Lujan, a member of the Taos Indian tribe. She spelled her married name "Luhan" rather than "Lujan" to help her English-speaking friends pronounce it.

After visiting the Taos area, Adams and Austin chose nearby Taos Pueblo as their subject. The pueblo was an Indian village with ancient roots, inhabited long before the Spanish reached America. Homes in the village were made of adobe, a mixture of mud and straw that blended into the landscape. Tony Lujan, a member of the pueblo's tribal council, helped the artists gain permission to work in the community.

Adams liked the clear southwestern light and photographed energetically. To be closer to the pueblo, he and Virginia sometimes stayed at Taos in one of the Luhan guesthouses. Despite a two-week break for surgery on a ruptured appendix, Adams finished his work and returned home in early June.

Back in San Francisco, Bender and Adams decided the book would be a limited edition of one hundred copies called *Taos Pueblo*, with fourteen pages of text by Austin and twelve photographs by Adams. As he had done for his first portfolio, Adams would hand-print each of the twelve hundred photographs.

Bender set the price at $75 per book, a high price at a time when many art books sold for $3.[2] (In $3 art books, the photographs were printed on a printing press; *Taos Pueblo* contained original photographs, handprinted by the photographer.) Bender showed his confidence in *Taos Pueblo* by ordering ten copies.

Church, Taos Pueblo, New Mexico, *by Ansel Adams.*

Austin's words and Adams's photographs blended well. The book received excellent artistic reviews, and all copies were sold within two years.[3]

Since their wedding, Ansel and Virginia had lived with her father in Yosemite or with his parents in San Francisco. In the first two years of marriage, Ansel's income from selling a few photographs and giving piano lessons was not enough to make a house payment. But he needed a real darkroom, not the makeshift one he had in his parents' basement. He also needed a large open area where he could practice piano and give lessons. Virginia wanted to have children, and she knew a home was a first step in that direction.[4]

By the winter of 1929–1930, Adams had begun to earn significant income from photography, particularly from sales of *Taos Pueblo*. In addition, early in 1930 the Yosemite Park and Curry Company (the successor to the company that had hosted Adams in tents years before) hired Adams to produce photographs promoting winter tourism. The contract was a great benefit to Adams and his family during the 1930s, a time of widespread unemployment and economic hardship in America. During the years of the Great Depression, Adams was able to earn $1,000 or more annually for a few months' work of taking and printing winter photographs. Meanwhile, millions of other men begged for jobs that paid $1 or $2 a day.[5]

But Ansel and Virginia still did not have enough money to buy a house. When his parents offered them a lot next to their own, a home became a reality. The young couple built a two-story house and dedicated it with a party in May 1930.

That same year, Ansel Adams returned to Taos looking for guidance on his career: Did his future lie in photography or music?[6] He and Virginia could not afford travel for two, so he traveled alone to Luhan's ranch. Luhan's guests at the time included the painter Georgia O'Keeffe. O'Keeffe's husband, Alfred Stieglitz, had stayed behind in New York City, where he maintained an important art gallery.

Another painter, John Marin, was also in residence. Marin was a friend of Stieglitz and O'Keeffe and his work was often featured in Stieglitz's gallery.[7] Like Edward Weston, Marin was won over by Adams's skill on the piano. When they first met, Marin saw Adams as a "tall thin man with a black beard. Laughing, stamping, making a noise." Marin did not particularly like him, but when Adams began to play the piano, Marin remarked, "Anybody who could make a sound like that I wanted for my friend always."[8]

Adams stayed in a guest house with Paul Strand, another friend of Stieglitz and O'Keeffe. In 1907 Strand and his high school camera club had visited a photo exhibit at Stieglitz's gallery, Strand was so moved by the black-and-white images that he chose photography as his profession.[9] In 1916 Stieglitz gave Strand a one-man show. In 1929 Strand raised money to help Stieglitz open a new gallery.[10]

One evening, Adams expressed an interest in seeing some of Strand's photographs. Strand said he had only negatives, but Adams still wanted to take a look. The next day, Strand brought out a box of four-inch-by-five-inch negatives. He placed a sheet of white paper in front of Adams and arranged the table so that the sun coming through a nearby window would pass through a negative and project a positive image onto the paper.

Adams was stunned by the straightforward images with clean lines and uncluttered edges. He also admired the beautiful, distinctive shapes and found the negatives "simple yet of great power."[11]

Strand's remarkable images convinced Adams to commit himself to photography.

With his course set, Adams's career began to unfold. In 1931 sixty of his photographs were displayed at the Smithsonian Institution in Washington, D.C. The next year, the M. H. de Young Memorial Museum in San Francisco presented eighty of his photographs. Adams also became photography critic for a San Francisco art journal. He reviewed works by Weston and by another Bay Area photographer, Imogen Cunningham. He praised their technique on clear close-ups of vegetables, flowers, and shells but criticized them when the elements were arranged in unnatural settings.[12]

In September 1932 Adams attended a meeting of a half dozen California photographers, including Weston and Cunningham, to discuss their art. Those present were aware of "pictorialism," a style of photography that used the camera to produce images similar to paintings. Models dressed in costumes to represent scenes from history, for example, or

The beard and broad-brimmed hat became Adams's trademarks.
This photo was taken in the Sierra Nevada in 1932.

photographers used soft-focus lenses to create a fuzzy, impressionist look.

Although they had used some of these techniques (particularly the soft-focus lens), Weston, Adams, and the others now rejected them. With prodding from Adams, the group agreed to commit itself to pure photography—that is, photography that works within the limits of the camera.

The crusaders called themselves Group f/64, named after one of the smallest lens settings available at that time. The f/64 setting gives a clear, highly detailed image. The group met only three or four times, but it did arrange an exhibit for its members at the de Young Museum for November 1932. The show featured eighty photographs, including ten by Adams, priced from $10 to $15 each.

The editor of *Camera Craft* magazine was impressed. Writing that although the "sharp focus, strong contrast, exaggerated highlighting, and bizarre subjects" took some getting used to, "these pictures do not sing. They shout."[13] Group f/64 was short-lived, but it encouraged its members to move to the forefront of artistic photography.

In early 1933, Virginia and Ansel learned that Virginia was pregnant. The baby was not due until August, and Virginia's father gave the couple $1,000 to use for travel in the meantime. Ansel and Virginia decided to go to New York City. In addition to seeing the sights, Ansel wanted to meet Alfred Stieglitz. And he had a few things he wanted Stieglitz to see.

Home and Away

On March 29, 1933, Ansel Adams stood in front of 509 Madison Avenue, New York City, carrying a portfolio of photographs. He entered the building, rode the elevator to the seventeenth floor, and opened a door marked AN AMERICAN PLACE. Alfred Stieglitz was in a back room.

Almost seventy years old, Stieglitz was a legend in the art world. He began making photographs in the 1880s and was the first to successfully photograph night scenes. In 1905 Stieglitz cofounded a small gallery that welcomed modern art from Europe and promoted photography as an art equal to painting. In 1929 he opened his own gallery—An American Place.

When Stieglitz emerged from the back room, Adams introduced himself. Stieglitz harshly dismissed the young photographer, telling him to come back in the afternoon. Adams returned to his wife, declaring that he wished to leave New York immediately. She urged him to try again.

In mid-afternoon, Adams reentered the gallery. This time Stieglitz agreed to see the portfolio. He carefully and silently examined each print. Adams waited in suspense. Finally Stieglitz pronounced: "Some of the finest photographs I've ever seen."[1]

Encouraged by his success with Stieglitz, Adams made other contacts in New York. He called on the owner of Delphic Studios and was able to arrange an exhibit there, his first in New York, for November 1933.

Adams also tried to visit Edward Steichen, Stieglitz's former ally in promoting photography as a fine art. Steichen had made his first photographs before 1900 and had done important work, but in the 1920s he had left creative photography for commercial work. At the time of Adams's visit, Steichen may have been the most financially successful photographer in America, doing fashion photography and portraits of wealthy individuals. Steichen, however, snubbed Adams, refusing to meet him.

Ansel and Virginia returned to California. In early July Ansel headed for the Sierra Club outing, leaving Virginia, who was eight months pregnant, at her father's home in Yosemite. Virginia gave birth to Michael Adams on August 1, 1933. Despite leaving camp a day early, Ansel did not make it back home until his son was two days old.

Adams's visits with Stieglitz had inspired him to

The legendary photographer Alfred Stieglitz, above, admired Adams's work as "some of the finest photographs I've ever seen."

start a gallery in San Francisco. After a few days with his wife and new son, Adams returned to San Francisco for the opening of his gallery. Edward Weston and other friends lent works, but sales at the gallery were weak. In the spring of 1934, Adams gave up on the gallery and turned it over to a friend.

Despite the gallery's failure, the winter of 1933–1934 held success for Adams. His exhibit at Delphic Studios in New York City was praised. A one-paragraph review in *The New York Times* reported that Adams's work "strikingly captures a world of poetic form. . . . It is masterly stuff."[2] In addition, Adams continued to earn $1,000 to $2,000 per year from the Yosemite Park and Curry Company for his winter photographs, which were printed on every-thing from menu covers to advertisements.

The spring of 1934 brought an election. Virginia had been on the board of directors of the Sierra Club in 1932, but when Michael was born in 1933, she resigned. Ansel and Virginia were both nominated for the 1934 election. As a frequent contributor to the club's magazine and a regular on the summer out-ings, Ansel was well known to club members. Virginia campaigned for Ansel, and Ansel campaigned for Virginia. Virginia did not win, but Ansel was elected to the board of directors of the Sierra Club, a post he would hold for thirty-seven years.

Adams's first mass-market book, *Making a Photograph*, was published in 1935. The how-to book explained all phases of photography, from taking a picture to designing a darkroom. *Making a Photograph* was a success and rapidly went into a second printing.

Adams sent a copy to Stieglitz, who responded with praise.

March of 1935 brought another addition to the Adams family with the birth of a daughter, Anne. Once again, Adams was absent for his child's birth. This time he was working on his contract for winter photographs of Yosemite.

At the end of 1935, Sierra Club leaders asked Adams to represent them in Washington, D.C. A proposal was before Congress to designate a large portion of Kings Canyon, where Adams had traveled in the summers of 1925 and 1926, as a national park. With the club paying most of his expenses, Adams would stop in New York City to enlist the help of other organizations committed to preserving wilderness areas. The trip would also provide an opportunity to visit Stieglitz.

Leaving Virginia and the children in California, Adams headed east in January 1936. In New York City, he called on Stieglitz with a portfolio of new photographs. Impressed, Stieglitz offered Adams an exhibition in November. He and Georgia O'Keeffe also introduced Adams to David McAlpin, a wealthy stockbroker with a growing interest in art.

In Washington, Adams entered a new world of politicians and lobbyists. He knew that William Henry Jackson's photographs had helped establish Yellowstone as the first national park. Adams hoped his own photographs of Kings Canyon would bring it to national park status. He gave a speech, making points with his photographs. He also met individually with politicians and government officials.

An unnamed peak, Kings River Canyon (Proposed as a National Park), California, *by Ansel Adams, ca. 1926.*

One of the officials he met was Harold Ickes. As U.S. secretary of the interior, Ickes was in charge of the national parks. He was impressed with Adams. Hearing that Adams had been working on large wall murals, Ickes took note. Kings Canyon would not become a national park until 1940, but Adams's photographs had given the movement a push in the right direction. In addition, Ickes would become an important friend.

On the way back to California, Adams stopped in Chicago to call on Katherine Kuh, owner of an influential art gallery. Kuh was ecstatic about Adams's photographs and offered him a fall exhibition. She promised that if he would attend the show, she would secure some commercial photography assignments for him in Chicago.

The fall of 1936 was going to be busy for Adams. The Stieglitz exhibition in New York City would begin October 27. The exhibit at the Kuh Gallery in Chicago would open a few days later.[3] He would have two major exhibitions occurring at the same time.

Meanwhile, Adams returned to San Francisco from the annual Sierra Club outing in August and retreated to his darkroom. He needed almost one hundred perfect photographic prints for the two exhibitions. By early October, the prints were finally finished.

On October 14, tragedy struck. Harry Best, Virginia's father, died of a heart attack. Three weeks later, Adams boarded a train heading east. It was a whirlwind trip. In Chicago he took portraits, photographed women's underwear for advertisements, lectured to the Chicago Camera Club, and made appearances at his exhibition.

Then he was off to New York, where he was stunned by the elegance of Stieglitz's gallery. He wrote to Virginia, "The show at Stieglitz is extraordinary . . . [the prints] are hung with the utmost style and selection."[4]

The exhibitions were financial successes. Many of the prints sold for $25 or $30, but in New York David McAlpin purchased a photograph of a white tombstone (Stieglitz's favorite) for $100.

Leaving New York, Adams traveled to Washington, D.C. There he met with the director of the National Park Service to confirm that Harry Best's permit to operate his store in Yosemite National Park could be passed on to Best's daughter. The director agreed to transfer the permit, allowing Virginia and Ansel Adams to operate what had become an important outlet for the sale of Ansel's photographs.

On the way home, Adams stopped in Chicago to take more commercial photographs. He returned to his family on December 10, 1936. In five weeks he had traveled a coast-to-coast loop by train: San Francisco to Chicago to New York to Washington, D.C., then back to Chicago and San Francisco. He was exhausted but triumphant.

Within six years of choosing his career, Adams had established himself as a major figure in American photography. He had mounted two exhibitions in New York City (Delphic Studios and Stieglitz), plus exhibitions in Washington, D.C. (Smithsonian Institution), Chicago (Kuh Gallery), and San Francisco (de Young Museum), and the Group f/64 exhibit, also at the de Young Museum. He had successfully released two sets of portfolios and published his first book. Critics praised his exhibitions, and he was starting to get a steady stream of commercial assignments.

But success exacted a price. The physical strain of his trip caused Adams to be hospitalized shortly after returning to San Francisco. He came home for Christmas, though he was still worn out in mind and body. In January, he was hospitalized again, for depression as well as a case of mononucleosis. Then, as he rested at home, an important letter arrived from Beaumont Newhall, a young art curator at the Museum of Modern Art in New York City.

Newhall was planning a major exhibition for 1937 entitled *Photography: 1839–1937*. In his letter, he asked Adams to lend some of his prints. Newhall's employer, the Museum of Modern Art (MoMA), had been founded in 1929 to showcase contemporary works of art ignored by traditional museums. Newhall's exhibition would be the first in the United States to present the full history and development of photography.[5] Adams was delighted to participate.[6] In addition to his own prints, he offered Newhall an album of photographs of the American Southwest taken by Timothy O'Sullivan in the 1870s.

MoMA's history of photography was a success. More than eight hundred photographs (including six by Adams) covered four floors of the museum. More than thirty thousand visitors toured the exhibit.[7] Adams was too ill to travel to New York, but he did see a smaller version of the collection in San Francisco that summer. The exhibition confirmed what he had known for years. "Photography is the most potent, the most direct, the most stimulating medium of human expression in this day," he wrote in a magazine article.[8]

Adams received more good news in the spring of 1937. His friend Edward Weston had received a fellowship from the Guggenheim Foundation, the first fellowship it awarded to a photographer. The foundation granted Weston $2,000 to travel and make photographs. Adams invited Weston to photograph the Sierra Nevada in July, when snow would be gone from the high elevation trails.

Weston and Adams had remained in close contact since their Group f/64 days. Weston was one of the first photographers to embrace straight, or pure, photography, and he had written the introduction to Adams's book *The Making of a Photograph.* What Adams called "visualization," Weston called "prevision." According to Weston, "One must prevision and feel, *before exposure,* the finished print. . . . Developing and printing become but a careful carrying on of the original conception."[9]

On July 20, Virginia and Ansel Adams welcomed Weston and his future wife, Charis Wilson, to Yosemite. Also joining the expedition would be Ron Partridge, who was the son of Group f/64 member Imogen Cunningham.

Partridge operated the darkroom at Best's Studio, developing vacationers' film as well as prints from Adams's negatives. Partridge's prints of Adams's photographs were labeled "special edition" photographs and sold in Best's Studio for a few dollars each. The same images, when printed by Adams, sold for $25 to $30 each in the galleries of Stieglitz and Kuh.

Leaving Virginia behind to mind the children and the store, the group traveled in the High Sierra for almost a week. Adams and Weston photographed independently but gathered for dinner at the end of each day.

Adams and his expedition returned to Best's Studio after dark on July 27, welcomed by Virginia with a chicken dinner. As they ate and discussed the trip, a cry went up: *"Fire!"* They looked outside to see yellow flames consuming Adams's darkroom. Everyone knew the most valuable items inside were the irreplaceable negatives. The tired campers rushed to the building. Some grabbed boxes of negatives. Someone grabbed a hose. Someone else grabbed a fire extinguisher. Steaming negatives were rushed into a bathtub filled with water.

When the guests had done all they could, drinks were passed around as Adams played Bach on the piano. He had lost about five thousand negatives, most of them work he had done for the Yosemite Park and Curry Company (YP&CC). The glass plate negative for *Monolith*, the striking photograph that was his first example of visualization, was saved, but it was seared across the top. For future prints, Adams was forced to crop the image to remove the damaged portion.

The loss of so many negatives contributed to Adams's loss of his annual contract with YP&CC. Each winter for seven of the previous eight years, the company had paid Adams $10 a day—more than

$1,000 a year—to produce photographs that could be used to promote winter vacations.

Adams's contract with the company stipulated that he would own the negatives. After the fire Adams received a payment from his insurance company, but YP&CC demanded that Adams replace each lost negative. Adams argued that he had fulfilled his contract to provide attractive images for advertising and public relations. Since most of the negatives had never been used, the total number of negatives was irrelevant. Two years later, in 1939, as a result of the dispute, Adams would end his relationship with the YP&CC, losing what had been his most reliable source of income.

Adams's sources of income, however, had already begun to diversify. In the spring of 1937, Walter Starr, a longtime Sierra Club member, approached Adams about doing photographs for a book in honor of Starr's son, Walter Jr. For years the young man had made notes in the Sierra Nevada, hoping to have them printed as a guidebook. Unfortunately, Walter Jr. died in a climbing accident. Starr had the book printed after his son's death, and he asked Adams to do photographs for an expanded edition.

Starr offered to pay the publishing costs and asked only that Adams make the final product first-class in every way. Adams selected prints from his files and added prints from his 1937 summer travels. When printing was about to begin, he inspected the photographic proofs. The proofs and the plates they were made from were not of the quality he wanted. With Starr's consent, and at Starr's expense, Adams instructed the printer to redo the plates. The result was a beautiful book, *Sierra Nevada: The John Muir Trail.*

Adams was proud of the book and sent a copy to Stieglitz, who replied, "You have literally taken my breath away. . . . What perfect photography."[10] Adams also sent a copy to the National Park Service in Washington. Secretary Ickes showed it to President Franklin D. Roosevelt, who admired the book so much that he kept it. In January 1939, the director of the National Park Service asked Adams to send Secretary Ickes another copy. Adams was delighted to do so.

In the Shadow of War

Ansel Adams's participation in Beaumont Newhall's photography exhibit at the Museum of Modern Art in 1937 was a wise investment. As a result of the exhibition, Adams gained two new friends, deepened his relationship with another friend, and received an important new appointment.

Adams corresponded with his new friends Beaumont and Nancy Newhall after the 1937 exhibition, but he did not actually meet them until a visit to New York in 1939. The following year the Newhalls visited Adams in California. During their stay, Beaumont revealed his plan for a photography department at MoMA. Adams supported the plan and offered to ask his friend David McAlpin for help. Not only was McAlpin wealthy, but he also had friends and relatives on the museum's board.[1]

At Adams's request, McAlpin lobbied for the new department. He also pledged a substantial donation. The museum's trustees agreed to start a department of photography and asked McAlpin to chair the advisory committee. McAlpin accepted the appointment, with Adams as his vice chairman. In addition, McAlpin agreed to personally pay Adams for his work.

Adams arrived in New York in October 1940 to help with the department's first exhibition. In his role as vice chairman, he spoke to professional photographers, seeking their support. He also met with businesses to raise money. Where necessary, he even printed photographs from other photographers' negatives to maintain the quality of the exhibit.

The December 1940 exhibit, *Sixty Photographs: A Survey of Camera Esthetics*, explored creative photography with examples from the museum's growing collection. Adams, Alfred Stieglitz, Edward Steichen, Paul Strand, and Edward Weston were all represented. Also included were works by Dorothea Lange and Walker Evans, two of the photographers hired by the government's Farm Service Administration to record the lives of Americans during the Great Depression of the 1930s. Mathew Brady and Timothy O'Sullivan were among eight deceased photographers honored.

Adams did not stay in New York for the opening of the exhibit. By mid-December he was back on the train, headed to Yosemite for Christmas and the year-end Bracebridge dinner.

When Adams returned to New York in April 1941,

war was in the air. Germany had conquered France, Belgium, and the Netherlands and was trying to crush England. The involvement of the United States seemed inevitable.

Adams suggested a MoMA competition for photographers, entitled *Images of Freedom,* to remind Americans of their values. Many photographers had recorded the poverty and suffering in America during the 1930s. Adams wanted a competition that would call on photographers to record America's positive ideals. Beaumont Newhall liked the idea. Nancy Newhall wrote an introduction asking photographers to record "our resources and our potential strength."[2]

The exhibit may have been an attempt by Adams to answer his critics. Some reviewers had complained that his photographs of trees and mountains were out of touch with human experience. The world had gone through ten years of a Great Depression and was entering a second world war. Yet those events were absent from Adams's work. French photographer Henri Cartier-Bresson (whose work was included in *Sixty Photographs*) said, "The world is going to pieces and people like Adams and Weston are photographing rocks!"[3]

Adams returned to his family in Yosemite for the summer. In late June he received a letter from the Department of the Interior indicating that Secretary Ickes wanted to talk to him about photographic murals—large pictures—for the walls of the department's office building. Adams was definitely interested. Here was a chance to present America's natural resources to the lawmakers and bureaucrats who decided which natural landscapes would be protected—and which would not.

In August Adams returned to New York to work on the MoMA competition. By the end of the month he was in Washington, D.C., to meet with Ickes about the murals. Ickes offered him the highest rate allowed for a government consultant—$22.22 per day, plus expenses—to travel and take pictures. According to the contract, Adams could work up to 180 days, photographing "Indian Reservations, national parks, and other places under the jurisdiction" of the Department of the Interior.[4] Additional fees would be paid for production of the murals from selected photos.

The contract from Secretary Ickes was perhaps the greatest commission of Adams's career. He would create an official portfolio of the national parks and other heritage sites of the United States. His rate would be more than double what Yosemite Park and Curry Company had paid him. He could also take days off to photograph other sites that interested him.

There was bad news with the good. While Ansel was in New York that summer, Virginia filed for divorce. She was tired of running Best's Studio and raising two children alone.[5]

Adams had made at least one trip to the East Coast each year since his first visit to see Stieglitz in 1933, but the first trip was the only one that had included Virginia. As his career progressed, the trips grew more frequent. In the eleven months before Virginia filed for divorce, Adams had made three trips east, each of them lasting a month or more. And, with the Department of the Interior contract, he would be

Navajo Woman and Infant, Canyon de Chelle, Arizona, *by Ansel Adams, ca. 1941. The Department of the Interior hired Adams to take photographs of the national parks, Indian reservations, and other heritage sites in the United States.*

away from his family again. Even when he was in California, Adams was often out touring with guests or camping with the Sierra Club.

Adams wrote Virginia from New York, pledging his love for his family. When he returned to California, some reconciliation was made and the divorce plans were dropped.

Adams prepared to leave to photograph the

Department of the Interior sites, taking Michael, his eight-year-old son, with him. Cedric Wright also joined the expedition. In mid-October, Ansel and Michael Adams and Cedric Wright headed for Arizona and New Mexico in a station wagon bursting with photographic equipment and camping gear.

Hoover Dam, Zion National Park, and the Grand Canyon were among their first stops. In Santa Fe, Adams reunited with old friends. Wright, however, soon tired of deserts and returned to California. Michael also had to leave the trip. Like his father twelve years before, Michael suffered an attack of appendicitis in New Mexico. He had surgery in the Carlsbad hospital, then recovered with friends while his father photographed mining operations for U.S. Potash.

Michael and Ansel were home by the end of November. On December 7, 1941, less than two weeks later, the Japanese bombed the U.S. naval base at Pearl Harbor, Hawaii, and the United States entered World War II. Adams realized the outbreak of war threatened his project. In late December 1941, Adams urged completion of the murals, writing to Ickes's assistant, "I believe my work relates most efficiently to an emotional presentation of 'what we are fighting for.'"[6]

Adams was too old for military duty, but Beaumont Newhall was not. When Newhall enlisted in the army as a photo intelligence officer, the museum appointed his wife, Nancy, acting curator. Adams, as vice chairman of the advisory committee, returned to New York to help Nancy Newhall.

Grand Teton National Park, Wyoming, *by Ansel Adams, ca. 1942. As the United States entered World War II, Adams believed that his photographs of the national parks would show Americans "what we are fighting for."*

Adams left New York in May to complete his photographs for the Department of the Interior. He traveled the northern portion of the western states by train, visiting Grand Teton, Yellowstone, Rocky Mountain, Glacier, and other national parks. By June he had most of the photographs he wanted, but he still had a great deal of work to do in the darkroom. The government agreed to an extension of his contract only for the purpose of printing the photographs. In November 1942 Adams completed the project. He sent Ickes 225 exhibition-quality prints of the national parks.[7]

During the war, the government lost interest in the murals, and they were never made. Adams's photographs sat on a shelf in the Department of the Interior until 1962, when the department sent the prints to the National Archives. There, they were ignored again. Finally, in 1988, Adams's prints were discovered by researchers. Soon after, they were published in a book and in posters commemorating the Mural Project.[8]

The Apple Orchard

After finishing the Mural Project, Adams tried to help with the war effort. He escorted troops through Yosemite Valley as they practiced mountaineering tactics, and he taught photography to soldiers at Fort Ord, south of San Francisco. At one point he worked under guard in an army darkroom to print top-secret photographs of Japanese military bases.

These assignments gave Adams little satisfaction, and he longed to do something that would be of more importance to the nation.[1] In 1942 he was pleased when Edward Steichen asked him to run a naval photo lab in Washington, D.C. Unfortunately, as it turned out, he lost out on this job. Steichen had snubbed Adams during his first visit to New York in 1933, and he insulted Adams again by quietly giving the naval post to someone else after Adams asked for time to finish the Mural Project.

In the summer of 1943, Adams expressed his frustration to Ralph Merritt, a friend from the Sierra Club. Merritt revealed that he had recently been appointed director of the War Relocation Camp at Manzanar, California, where thousands of Japanese Americans were being held. He invited Adams to photograph conditions there.

Ansel Adams, Wildcat Hill, 1943. *The famed photographer Edward Weston took this picture of his friend Ansel Adams.*

Shortly after Japan attacked Pearl Harbor, several political and military leaders had called for the removal of persons of Japanese descent from the coastal states of California, Oregon, and Washington. They worried that some Japanese Americans might try to aid Japan. Because it would be impossible to separate loyal from disloyal, they argued that all Japanese Americans should be removed. Others claimed that Japanese Americans should be removed to protect them from angry neighbors.

On February 19, 1942, President Roosevelt signed an order permitting military commanders in the United States to establish areas for relocation camps.[2] A month later, the commander of the Western Defense Command ordered the evacuation of families of Japanese descent in the West Coast states.

Some families had as few as four days in which to report to control stations for removal.[3] They were allowed to bring only personal items that they could carry. In most cases they were forced to sell their homes and businesses, sometimes getting only a tenth of their value. Eventually, more than 112,000 Japanese Americans were evacuated to ten relocation camps, also known as internment camps. Two-thirds of those removed were United States citizens; one-fourth were children under fifteen years of age.[4]

The first camp to receive Japanese Americans was Manzanar in the Owens Valley of California, east of the Sierra Nevada. *Manzanar* is the Spanish word for "apple orchard." In reality, Manzanar was a prison. Barbed wire surrounded it. Guard towers with searchlights and machine guns stood at each corner. Ten thousand people lived in wooden army barracks, with bathrooms and showers in separate buildings. Families ate in mess halls.

The prisoners tried to make the best of a terrible situation. Many of the Japanese Americans were farmers. In prison they planted crops, revitalized the orchards, and raised chickens and pigs. Eventually they produced enough food to feed themselves and to sell on the open market.

Other prisoners represented every profession found in a small town. Doctors, dentists, and nurses provided medical care. Carpenters made improvements in the camp. Editors and reporters started a newspaper. Shopkeepers opened a department store. Teachers opened schools.

Besides going to school, young people had a variety of activities. They played baseball and volleyball. They could join Girl Scout and Boy Scout units. Churches and a YMCA chapter also offered programs.

The situation, however, was not rosy, nor was it always peaceful. A few days after Merritt assumed control, a riot broke out. When the crowd refused to disperse, guards opened fire, killing two men.[5] Over time, the atmosphere calmed down as Merritt and the Japanese-American leaders learned to work together.

Adams was interested in photographing the camp, though he was not the first to do so. Dorothea Lange, whom Adams had met through Albert Bender, was among a group of photographers hired by the War Relocation Authority to record the relocation process.

Dorothea Lange took this picture in Centerville, California, in 1942. On the wall behind the mother and baby are schedules listing the names of Japanese American families and their bus assignments.

Lange photographed families packing, waiting at assembly areas, and being transported. She also photographed the early days of the Manzanar camp.

When Adams arrived at Manzanar in the fall of 1943, the camp had been in operation for almost a year and a half. He returned periodically through the winter of 1943–1944, bringing Virginia with him on at least one visit. It was from Manzanar that he and Virginia left to photograph *Winter Sunrise, the Sierra Nevada, from Lone Pine.*

Adams was allowed to photograph at Manzanar as he wished, but he was forbidden to photograph the guard towers and the barbed wire fences. Adams said that his goal was to demonstrate how, "with admirable strength of spirit," the Japanese Americans had "made a life for themselves, a unique micro-civilization under difficult conditions."[6]

He photographed all aspects of camp life—people working in the fields, lining up for meals, at choir practice, in the co-op store, and even at a town hall meeting. He made family and individual portraits. And he took landscape photographs that showed the camp with the Sierra Nevada in the background.

Farm Workers, Mount Williamson in background, Manzanar, *by Ansel Adams, ca. 1943.*

Adams found it especially disturbing to photograph young men and women in their military uniforms who had come home on leave.[7] These young people had enlisted to defend the United States, the very nation that had imprisoned their parents, brothers, and sisters on suspicion of being disloyal.

Adams wrote to Nancy Newhall in New York City about his project. Working together, she and Adams prepared an exhibit of Manzanar photographs for the Museum of Modern Art. Adams entitled the exhibit *Born Free and Equal: The Story of Loyal Japanese Americans.* He included a statement from Abraham Lincoln regarding the hypocrisy of discrimination in a nation that proclaimed, "All men are created equal."[8] The museum's board was reluctant to approve the exhibit and twice canceled it. Finally, the museum allowed the exhibit after the quote from Lincoln was deleted and the title changed to *Manzanar: Photographs by Ansel Adams of Loyal Japanese Relocation Center.*[9]

After the MoMA exhibit, Adams was able to get his photographs, as well as Lincoln's comment, published in a book with the *Born Free and Equal* title. In the book Adams stated his feelings about the importance of nature:

> In these years of strain and sorrow, the grandeur, beauty, and quietness of the mountains are more important to us than ever before. . . . the acrid splendor of the desert, ringed with towering mountains, has strengthened the spirit of the people of Manzanar.[10]

School children, Manzanar, *by Ansel Adams, ca. 1943. Adams wanted to capture the "admirable strength of spirit" of the Japanese Americans in the camps.*

Despite his objections to the relocation program, Adams avoided criticizing the government. His comments focused on the positive accomplishments of the Japanese Americans.

When Dorothea Lange saw Adams's photographs in *Born Free and Equal,* she thought his work was "shameful," failing to capture the injustice of the situation.[11] Even though she had worked as a government employee, Lange was outraged by what she saw. She tried to reveal the tragedy in her photographs.

Adams and Lange did have one factor in common. The photographs they made at Manzanar became the property of the American people. Lange worked for a government agency. Today, her photographs are available in the National Archives. Adams worked only for himself at Manzanar, but to assure that the nation would not forget what happened there, he donated all but a few of his Manzanar negatives to the Library of Congress.

At the end of the war, the camps were closed. Some Japanese Americans never returned to the West Coast, moving to the East Coast or the Midwest instead. Even those who returned home had to start from scratch. In many cases they had lost their possessions, their houses, and their jobs. Payments were made in 1948, 1951, and 1965 to reimburse evacuees for their losses, but the payments often amounted to less than 10 percent of actual losses.[12]

In 1988 the president of the United States signed a law apologizing, on behalf of the nation, to all Japanese Americans who were imprisoned. In addition, the law authorized a payment of $20,000 to every person relocated to the camps who was still living. Unfortunately, approximately sixty thousand of those relocated had died by 1988, and no payment was made to their descendants.

A Photographer at Work

The years after World War II marked one of the most diverse and productive periods of Ansel Adams's career. Creative photography, commercial assignments, exhibitions, publishing, and teaching were all part of Adams's growing importance as an American artist.

Despite his increasing success, Adams continued to be irritated by Edward Steichen's endeavors. In 1942, while Beaumont Newhall was away on military duty, the Museum of Modern Art had invited Steichen to present a photography exhibition on the war effort. Steichen's *Road to Victory* was a great success. Adams, however, believed the exhibit was propaganda, not art, and that the museum should be reserved for works of art. In Adams's opinion, the exhibit would have been more appropriate in an arena like Madison Square Garden.[1] Later in the war, Steichen organized another MoMA exhibit on a patriotic theme, *Power in the Pacific.*

In 1946, without consulting the photography advisory committee (which included Adams), the MoMA trustees appointed Steichen director of the museum's department of photography. Steichen offered to allow Newhall to stay on, but it was clear that Newhall would report to Steichen. With Adams's encouragement, Newhall resigned. Adams, David McAlpin, and the museum's entire photography advisory committee soon resigned in support of Newhall.[2]

While the feud with Steichen and the MoMA trustees was unfortunate, Adams was ready to move on. He wanted to complete his photographs of the national parks. Harold Ickes had left the federal government, and funding from that source was unlikely. Adams applied instead to the Guggenheim Foundation. The foundation had funded Edward Weston in 1937–1938 and later gave money to Dorothea Lange and Walker Evans. In April 1946 the foundation awarded Adams $3,000 to complete his photographs of the national parks and monuments.

Among those congratulating Adams on the grant was Alfred Stieglitz, who wrote, "If anyone ever earned the Guggenheim you did." That was Stieglitz's last letter to Adams.[3] Stieglitz died July 13, 1946. While Adams would continue to benefit from the friendship of McAlpin, the Newhalls, and others, Stieglitz was his last mentor. Adams had eagerly learned from a series of teachers. After Stieglitz, it was Adams's turn to become the teacher and mentor of others.

In 1946, however, Adams's first priority was to take advantage of his Guggenheim grant. He bought a Cadillac station wagon and installed his photographic platform on top.[4] In December, he attended the Bracebridge dinner at Yosemite, and then, in January 1947, he headed south. His first stops were Death Valley and Joshua Tree National Monuments in California. Then he went to Organ Pipe Cactus and Saguaro in Arizona, and finally to White Sands National Monument and Carlsbad Caverns National Park in New Mexico. In May, with Nancy and Beaumont Newhall in tow, Adams visited Zion and Bryce Canyon National Parks in Utah.

When it came to cameras, Adams never traveled lightly. Although good-quality smaller cameras were becoming available, he favored the larger negatives and the precision available from large cameras. Nancy Newhall recalled that on their trip to Bryce Canyon, in addition to camping gear and sleeping bags for three, Adams filled the car with four large cameras, three tripods, three lenses, four filter sets, and many other camera gadgets.[5] In later years, when students asked what camera he used, Adams would reply, "The heaviest one I can carry!"[6]

The Guggenheim grant would be a better business deal for Adams than the agreement with Ickes had been. Under Adams's contract with the Department of the Interior, the government (and therefore the public) owned the rights to the photographs from the Mural Project. Adams could print copies of the photographs,

Cactus and Surrounding Shrubs in "Saguaro National Monument," Arizona, *by Ansel Adams, ca. 1941.*

but so could anyone else. Under the Guggenheim grant, Adams would hold exclusive rights to his photographs, including copyright. This difference became important as Adams's popularity grew.

In the short run, however, the Guggenheim grant paid little more than the cost of Adams's travel and photographic expenses. Adams had two families to support—Virginia and the children in Yosemite and his elderly mother and father in San Francisco.

In the postwar years, Adams alternated between his personal, creative photography (which he called "assignments from 'within'") and the more profitable, commercial assignments ("assignments from 'without'").[7] Among his commercial assignments, Adams did work for *Fortune* magazine and sold color images to Standard Oil Company for its promotions.

One of Adams's favorite clients was Eastman Kodak. The company was constantly trying to promote photography by encouraging the public to take pictures. The company liked showing pictures of people taking pictures in its promotions. Usually the couple or family in Adams's photograph for Kodak would be looking at, and photographing, some natural wonder, such as a waterfall.

Adams also felt a need to keep publishing. In 1948 he published *Yosemite and the Sierra Nevada*, which included the writings of John Muir and sixty photographs by Adams. He also started a series of books on photographic technique that were an expansion of his 1935 book, *Making a Photograph*. In 1948 he published two books, *Camera and Lens* and *The Negative*. In 1950 he added *The Print*. These books became the basis for Adams's classic how-to series on photography. He revised the books over the years to keep up with changes in technology, as well as to include input from other photographers and scientists. Even today, the series is still available.

In 1948 Adams also decided to do a portfolio of his recent work. It had been a dozen years since *Taos Pueblo*, and that work had limited him to a single subject. The new portfolio, called simply *Portfolio One*, had twelve carefully printed photographs and was limited to seventy-five copies. Adams dedicated it to Alfred Stieglitz. Defending Stieglitz's concept of photography as fine art, Adams wrote,

> *A true photograph need not be explained . . . my photo-graphs are presented here as ends in themselves, images of the endless moments of the world.*[8]

Other than a 1938 portrait of Stieglitz at work over his desk, all photographs in *Portfolio One* are from 1946 or 1948. Only two are of Yosemite. The subject matter of the others ranges from a saguaro cactus in Arizona to a Mormon temple in Utah. The portfolios quickly sold at $100 each.

The Guggenheim Foundation renewed Adams's grant in 1948 to allow him to complete his national parks project. In all, he made 2,250 images of the national parks on his Guggenheim-sponsored travels. He also had six hundred images he had made for the Mural Project.[9] In 1950 he organized the best of these into a book, *My Camera in the National Parks*, and he offered *Portfolio Two: The National Parks and Monuments*, dedicated to Albert Bender. For the first time, eastern parks were included in his work, with photographs of Great Smoky Mountains National Park in Tennessee and Acadia National Park in Maine.

While Adams preferred to photograph alone, his commercial assignments resulted in some interesting work with Dorothea Lange. When Adams had first met Lange in the late 1920s, she was a successful portrait photographer in the Bay Area. With the onset of the Great Depression in the 1930s, Lange had left her studio to photograph life around her. During the Depression she was one of the photographers hired by the Farm Security Administration (FSA) to record the struggle of America's farm families.

Despite their differences about the camp at Manzanar, Adams and Lange worked together on other projects during World War II. The Office of War Information (OWI), an agency that assembled information about the United States to be sent overseas, sponsored one of these projects. Working for the OWI, Adams and Lange did a series of photographs in San Francisco. They took pictures of Italian Americans exercising their freedom, such as freedom of speech. Eventually the photographs were incorporated into a magazine that was dropped into Italy ahead of advancing American combat units.

In 1944 editors of *Fortune* magazine asked Adams and Lange to do a story on the problems that rapid growth had brought to the town of Richmond, California. Adams and Lange agreed that she would do portraits and up-close work, while he would do landscapes and big-picture work. Later the magazine

Adams was hired to work with photographer Dorothea Lange, above, on a variety of projects.

asked them to do a photo essay on California farming. Since *Fortune* was a business magazine, the editors were interested in the problems faced by corporate farms. True to her FSA experience, Lange wanted to focus on families struggling on small farms. Adams understood that this was an assignment from "without" and tried to give *Fortune* what it wanted.[10]

Lange became seriously ill in the early 1950s, but by 1953 she had recovered enough to take on another project with Adams. They would photograph Mormon communities in Utah. Adams was eager to take more pictures of people. After the Italian-American project, he had written to David McAlpin, "The work I did with Dorothea Lange is right up my alley. . . . I am interested in people and I feel that I shall do increasingly intense work with human subjects."[11]

Lange got a preliminary commitment from *Life* to use the Mormon photographs in a story. The popular weekly magazine was known for articles featuring outstanding black-and-white photographs. Lange and her husband, Paul Taylor, met with Mormon church elders to seek permission to photograph three small towns. The Mormons were suspicious and untrusting of outsiders, but Taylor, a professor of economics, gave the project credibility as a serious study. He and Lange told the church elders about the possibility of a traveling exhibition of photographs. They said nothing about an article in *Life* magazine.

Two weeks into the project, Adams discovered that Lange and Taylor had not told the Mormons about the possibility of a story in *Life*. According to Adams, every time he suggested they tell the Mormons the truth, Lange threatened to quit and go home.[12]

After completing their photography, Adams and Lange returned to California and prepared boards with 135 pictures presenting the Mormons' story. In the spring of 1954, Lange took the boards to New York. Impressed, the editors at *Life* promised a cover photo with an eighteen-page story, enough space for about seventy photographs.

The photo essay "Three Mormon Towns" appeared in the September 6, 1954, issue of *Life* magazine. Despite the editors' promises, however, the Mormons were pushed off the cover by photographs of fashions from Paris. Inside the magazine, the editors reduced the story to ten pages with thirty-five photographs. The smallest of the three towns, Toquerville, was made to seem like a ghost town. Two photographs featured a house with broken windows. The caption read, "Toquerville is old and quiet but its children have gone away."[13] The other two towns received a fair but skimpy report.

Many Mormon leaders were furious about the story in *Life*. One woman from Toquerville threatened to sue. Adams was unhappy that neither he nor Lange had told the Mormons the truth. He wrote to Nancy Newhall, "I am embarrassed by having something to do with what I think was an unethical business."[14]

What could have been a great success became a disappointment for Adams. Afterward, he avoided documentary projects and collaboration with other photographers. Instead, he returned to photographs of landscapes and still objects, subjects that did not require permission.

A few months after publication of "Three Mormon Towns," Adams received a request from Edward Steichen, still the director of photography at the Museum of Modern Art. Steichen was planning an exhibit called *The Family of Man*, featuring photographers from around the world. The exhibit would explore universal themes like love, work, war, and peace.

Steichen wanted to include Adams's photograph *Mount Williamson, From Manzanar, California, 1944*, a picture taken during Adams's visits to the Manzanar relocation camp. In this view of Mount Williamson in the Sierra Nevada, the mountain peak rises above a rugged and boulder-strewn foreground.

Adams was reluctant to send Steichen a negative. He preferred to produce the mural-size print to his own specifications. Steichen insisted on a print by his staff so that the tone would match the tone of other prints in the exhibition. Adams reluctantly sent a duplicate negative.

When Adams visited the exhibit, his fears were confirmed: *Mount Williamson* was poorly printed. Also, many other prints in the exhibition had been enlarged beyond the limits of quality. Adams felt the show would have been ideal for the United Nations but had no place in an art museum.[15]

Whether Adams liked him or not, Steichen was an important force in American photography. Steichen had been exhibiting photographs since before Adams was born, and he had excelled at every phase of his photographic career: pictorialism, pure photography, and portraits. In addition, beginning with *Road to Victory* and continuing through *The Family of Man*, Steichen was the master of blockbuster photo exhibits.

Adams and Steichen approached photography from different perspectives. Adams firmly believed that the highest form of photography was art, a view Steichen had abandoned. Late in his life Steichen observed: "When I first became interested in photography . . . my idea was to have it recognized as one of the fine arts. Today I don't give a hoot . . . about that. The mission of photography is to explain man to man and each to himself."[16]

Steichen's *Family of Man* was the most widely seen exhibition of photography up to its time, and millions of copies of the book edition were sold. The show included 503 photographs by 273 photographers from 68 nations.[17] And, while Adams may have felt his picture did not receive the quality printing it deserved, it was treated with respect. Adams's photograph is one of only three in the book that receives a full two-page spread.

Despite his objections to *Family of Man*, Adams was not opposed to exhibits that showcased works by a variety of photographers on a single theme. In 1954 the Park Service told the Sierra Club that it had to make wider use of the LeConte Memorial Lodge. Adams and Nancy Newhall came to the rescue, suggesting an exhibition to promote conservation. In 1955 they presented *This Is the American Earth*, with text by Newhall. Most of the photographs were by Adams, but thirty-two other photographers were

Ansel Adams, *ca. 1948, in Alaska. As his popularity grew, Adams alternated between personal, creative photography and commercial assignments that paid well.*

included. Like Steichen, Adams insisted that each photographer send him a negative from which he could print a photograph in the appropriate size and tones. And, like Steichen's *Family of Man*, Adams's show was a hit and was sent on tour throughout the world.

In 1955 Adams also began a series of photography workshops in Yosemite National Park. This was not his first teaching experience. As early as 1940, Adams had served as an instructor at the Art Center School of Los Angeles. It was there he developed the "zone system" for helping photographers regulate the amount of light allowed to reach the film.

The Ansel Adams Workshops in Yosemite National Park were his most successful teaching venture. He conducted them each summer from 1955 to 1981. In all, he personally instructed more than forty-five hundred students.[18] Many of them would become outstanding professional photographers.

"Remember Tenaya!!!"

During the 1950s, Adams's reputation as a photographer continued to grow. He took on commercial assignments from Pacific Gas and Electric, Kennecut Copper, Paul Mason Vineyards, Hills Brothers Coffee, *Fortune* magazine, and others. In addition, he became a consultant to the Polaroid Corporation, makers of the Polaroid Land camera and innovators in the field of instant photography. Adams would be a Polaroid consultant for more than thirty years.

Adams also continued his involvement with the Sierra Club. He had been a member of the Sierra Club board since his election in 1934 and he championed a number of Sierra Club causes, but he was not afraid to stand alone if necessary.

In 1956 the National Park Service proposed building new roads to make the parks more accessible. Many Sierra Club members worried that new roads would fill the parks with more visitors and would allow crowds of tourists to reach wilderness areas formerly available only to backpackers.

Despite their concerns about overcrowding, Sierra Club board members found it difficult to oppose additional roads. Years earlier, William Colby had suggested that people should go to the woods to "hear the trees speak for themselves."[1] And one of the original reasons for founding the Sierra Club had been to "render accessible the mountain regions."[2]

Adams said that "wilderness with a slick highway through it is no longer wild."[3] He was particularly concerned about a new road in Yosemite Park near Tenaya Lake. To build the road, plans called for blasting away granite rock that had been polished by glaciers over thousands of years. Adams pointed out that a road built on soil could be removed and trees and grass would eventually regrow. The scar made by dynamiting granite rock would be permanent.[4]

In 1958, when the Sierra Club failed to take a stand against the new road, Adams submitted his resignation. He then sent angry telegrams to the director of the National Park Service and to the secretary of the interior condemning the blasting and calling it an act "which approaches criminal negligence."[5] Within a few days, Adams met with the superintendent of Yosemite National Park and offered an alternative route. Despite his forceful one-man campaign, the blasting was done and the road went through. Adams was so upset that he had a rubber stamp made exclaiming, "Remember Tenaya!!!" and often used it on his personal mail.[6]

Adams also lost on another front: The Sierra Club board rejected his resignation. Friends convinced him that his strong voice for wilderness preservation was needed, and he agreed to continue as a board member.

Among those who urged Adams to continue was his friend David Brower. Brower had met Adams in Yosemite in 1933. Shortly after that, Brower became publicity director for the Yosemite Park and Curry Company. His duties included sending Adams's winter photographs of Yosemite to newspapers. In 1952 Adams endorsed Brower as the Sierra Club's first executive director. When the Sierra Club published volume one of Adams's authorized biography, *Ansel Adams, The Eloquent Light* by Nancy Newhall, Brower wrote in the foreword, "It's hard to tell which has shaped the other more—Ansel Adams or the Sierra Club."[7]

In 1959 Adams received a third fellowship from the Guggenheim Foundation, this one to support him while he printed his photographs. In his work with his cameras, he often lacked the time to print photographs to his strict standards. In 1960, Adams created *Portfolio Three: Yosemite Valley*. While the portfolio continued Adams's tradition of spectacular images dramatically printed, it was also a hint that Adams's most productive years of capturing images were behind him. Of the sixteen images in the portfolio, not one was from the previous four years and only six were based on photographs taken in the 1950s. The other ten photographs had been taken between 1927 and 1948.

The year 1961 brought more change. For thirty years, Adams's home had been the small two-story house that he and Virginia had built in San Francisco. With the death of his parents in the early 1950s, Ansel inherited their home, adjacent to his. Both homes were out of date, and his basement darkroom was inadequate for the growing demand for his photographs. A wealthy friend offered Adams a hillside parcel in Carmel, 120 miles south of San Francisco. The scenic lot overlooked the Pacific Ocean. Adams accepted, hiring an architect to draw up plans for a house. He and Virginia moved into their spacious new home in 1962.

The 1960s were years of social and political upheaval, and the Sierra Club, with Ansel Adams as a board member, was increasingly involved in battles to preserve wilderness areas. One of the most significant battles was over a government proposal in 1964 to lease fifteen thousand acres of the Mineral King National Forest, near Sequoia National Park, to the Disney Corporation for a ski resort. The resort would include lodging for three thousand visitors and an access road through Sequoia National Park.

The plan was controversial even inside the Sierra Club. Many club members were avid skiers, and the club's board had supported a proposal for a ski resort at Mineral King in 1949. While some board members believed they could not go against an earlier decision, younger members pointed out that the proposed resort was significantly larger than the one imagined fifteen years earlier.

Even though he was a close friend of the board members who argued for no change in policy, Adams opposed the resort. Remembering his loss at Tenaya Lake, he would not allow a new road through a national park, and in 1965 he joined with the majority of the board in repealing their consent. When three club chapters protested the decision and endorsed development, Adams counseled club leaders to stand firm.[8] Eventually Disney Corporation gave up the idea, and the area was incorporated into Sequoia National Park.

Adams and the Sierra Club won another victory in the 1960s, defeating a proposal to place dams just above and below the Grand Canyon in Arizona. While the dams would not flood Grand Canyon National Park, they would flood parts of the canyon outside the Park. The Sierra Club opposed the dams, but politicians and developers favored them because they would bring water and electricity to Phoenix. Some supporters also pointed to the lakes that would be created for recreation.

In July 1966, Adams wrote Brower that flooding the Grand Canyon for recreation would be like flooding the Sistine Chapel so that tourists could get a better look at the painted ceiling. Later that summer, without Adams's prior knowledge, Brower ran a full page ad in *The New York Times* with the headline "SHOULD WE ALSO FLOOD THE SISTINE CHAPEL SO TOURISTS CAN GET NEARER THE CEILING?"[9] There was a public outcry, and six months later the administration

Grand Canyon from South Rim, 1941, Arizona, *by Ansel Adams.*

of President Lyndon Johnson announced it would oppose the dams.

The ad was one of the club's most influential ever, generating public support and new members. Adams, however, was unhappy with Brower's confrontational tactics. While he took strong stands, Adams favored resolving issues by negotiation rather than conflict. He believed, "You don't get anywhere by kicking people in the shins when you should be sitting down around the table."[10]

Adams and Brower were soon on opposite sides of a bitter Sierra Club battle over the placement of a nuclear power plant along California's Pacific Coast. Originally, Pacific Gas and Electric (PG&E) had proposed a power plant for Nipomo Dunes, a scenic area Adams had photographed and some Sierra Club members had targeted as a state park. In 1966, Adams and a few of the club's leaders convinced PG&E to transfer the proposed site to another, less important coastal location—Diablo Canyon. Brower and other board members opposed the compromise, believing the club should not surrender one natural area to save another.

The battle raged for three years. In 1967 Adams recommended that Brower be dismissed for his aggressive policies, for failing to follow board direction, and for poor management of club publishing ventures and finances. The board curtailed Brower's authority but allowed him to stay.

The conflict came to a head in the 1969 Sierra Club elections. Brower led a slate of five members who pledged to support more aggressive programs.

Five other members, including Adams, promised sound management and progress through cooperation, not confrontation. Brower had sufficient board support to deny Adams the nominating committee endorsement for the first time since his election in 1934.[11]

In the balloting, Adams and his group captured all five available spots. The board accepted Brower's resignation at its next meeting. As many as a dozen members of the staff who had supported Brower quickly resigned or were dismissed.

Adams had won the election, but it was his last one. In 1971, after thirty-seven years of service, he resigned from the board of the Sierra Club. At age sixty-nine, Adams was in declining health. He believed the club needed younger leadership.[12]

Over the years, the Sierra Club had been Adams's employer, his mentor, his inspiration, and his publisher. In turn, he had been its photographer, its trail guide, its voice, and, at times, its conscience.

Artist Triumphant

Ansel Adams continued to take photographs throughout his life, but after 1965 he recorded few new artistic images.[1] Carrying a large camera with all its accessories into wild places was work for a younger man. In addition, Adams had created thousands of negatives over his lifetime. He did not need more images. He needed to print and market the images he had.

In April 1971 Adams hired William Turnage as his manager. Turnage was straight out of the Yale University School of Forestry. The two men had similar views on wilderness conservation, and Adams admired Turnage's business sense. Their strategy was that Turnage would relieve Adams of many of his business chores while at the same time increasing his income.

Turnage and Adams launched a variety of plans. The first was an agreement with the University of Arizona to establish the Center for Creative Photography. Under the agreement, upon Adams's death, the center would receive and care for his negatives, making them available to scholars. Although the plan did not directly earn money for Adams, it relieved his concerns about the fate of the thousands of negatives that were his life's work.

Another agreement did make money for Adams. This was a contract with the New York Graphic Society, a division of Little, Brown and Company, as exclusive publisher of Adams's books. The contract not only gave Adams significant royalties (a portion of sales) but also gave him the power to select the designer, the printer, and the paper that would be used for the books.[2] Beginning with his first portfolio, Adams had insisted on quality work, and he was not about to let quality slip in the world of mass-market publications.

In 1974 the Metropolitan Museum of Art in New York City hosted Adams's first solo museum show in New York. Adams's old friend David McAlpin arranged the exhibition and provided some of the funding. The 156 images in the Metropolitan show included a wide range of Adams's photographs, plus work he had done with the Polaroid camera.

Critics were divided on the value of the exhibit. A *New York Times* reviewer wrote that Adams had lost touch with nature in his quest for perfect prints:

> *The very perfection that Mr. Adams brings to every print—a technical perfection for which he has few peers—contributes, moreover, to a certain air of unreality in his work. . . . In the end it isn't nature that one responds to so much as the craft of the darkroom.*[3]

Another reviewer admired the qualities of an Adams print:

> *Hardened professionals grow silent with awe at Adams's ability to hold the detail in the darkest shadows, even up against the very brightest lights . . .*[4]

Adams and Turnage also devised a plan to help Adams clean up a backlog of print orders and free him from long hours in the darkroom. In the spring of 1975, Turnage announced that Adams would no longer accept print orders after December 31, 1975. Prints of sixteen inches by twenty inches would be sold for $800. Adams's most popular image, *Moonrise, Hernandez, New Mexico*, would sell for $1,200.[5]

The plan increased Adams's bank account and his workload. By the end of 1975, more than three thousand orders had been received. The value of the orders approached $2 million. It would take years to complete all this work. Adams already had one darkroom assistant, and he hired a second.

Adams was in charge of printing each image, but the assistants handled many of the routine chores. Despite all the technological advances, printing photographs still resembled chemistry as much as artistry. A drop of water, a speck of dust, or a flaw in the paper could ruin a day's work. On a particularly

Adams poses in front of Moonrise, Hernandez, New Mexico. *This 1941 photograph became one of his most popular images and his highest-priced photograph.*

awful day, one of Adams's assistants discovered small bubbles in copies of *Winter Sunrise*. Adams ordered the destruction of almost one hundred marred prints—a week's work.[6]

Two trends carried Adams to success. One was an interest in photography as art. Traditional arts such as painting were escalating in cost beyond the range of many investors. Photography was affordable, and in a nation surrounded by television and photography magazines, photographic art seemed natural.

At the same time, Americans were becoming more interested in the wilderness and their natural heritage. People were flocking to the national parks. In 1978, 2.7 million people visited Yosemite.[7] These visitors wanted to bring the outdoor experience into their homes. What better way than an Ansel Adams book or photograph? By 1979 Adams had more than one million books in print, and original Adams photographs were selling for as much as $8,000 each.[8]

Adams himself rarely received the top prices for his art. By the time he filled his three-thousand–plus orders for photographs, many of those photographs were selling on the collectors' market at five to ten times Adams's price of $800.

Adams's popularity also brought reconciliation with the Museum of Modern Art. In 1979 MoMA hosted an exhibition of Ansel Adams landscapes called *Ansel Adams and the West*. The exhibit included early prints and late prints from the same negatives, demonstrating the change in Adams's technique over the years. The early prints were more subtle. The late prints showed dramatic contrasts between blacks and whites. When asked about the changes, Adams explained, "I like my prints full of beans now. I guess I get more belligerent as I get older."[9]

The exhibition was a triumph, complete with a *Time* magazine cover story and a new book, *Yosemite and the Range of Light*.

Adams's success even spread to the White House. When President Gerald R. Ford invited him to the White House in 1975, Adams came bearing an original print and an eight-point memorandum for improvement of the national parks. In 1979 the National Gallery asked Adams to do the official portrait of President Jimmy Carter, the first portrait of a U.S. president done by photograph. Since Adams was not a portrait specialist, he decided to use a Polaroid camera, producing images that could be evaluated immediately. Adams's friends at Polaroid gladly lent a camera capable of creating a twenty-by-twenty-four-inch image. The presidential portrait was a success. Adams made four good images: one each for the gallery, the president, Polaroid, and himself.[10] The next year, President Carter awarded Adams the Presidential Medal of Freedom, the nation's highest civilian honor.

Adams's relationship with the White House was not always cordial, however. Ronald Reagan, a former California governor, defeated Carter in the 1980 presidential election. Adams believed that as governor, Reagan did "what he was advised or ordered to do by the wealthy ruling factions to which he was so beholden."[11] When a magazine asked Adams to go to Santa Barbara to photograph Reagan, Adams refused.[12]

President Gerald R. Ford, right, invited Adams to visit the White House in 1975.

In 1983 Adams sat for a lengthy magazine interview. Speaking of Reagan administration budget cuts that forced painters in a university art department to fight with photographers over reduced dollars, Adams lifted his martini glass and said, "I'd like to drown him in here."[13] Adams was equally critical of Reagan policies that opposed placing more land under federal protection. "It is horrifying that we have to fight our own government to save our environment," said Adams. "Our worst enemy is the person the President designated with the responsibility of managing the country's environment: James Watt."[14] (Watt was Reagan's secretary of the interior.)

Not long after the interview appeared in print, a

call came to Adams's office. President Reagan wanted to meet with him. The two men spoke at a hotel suite in Beverly Hills, California. Adams found Reagan to be friendly, but their views differed. Adams accused James Watt of being "the most dangerous man in the country today" and urged the president to protect more natural areas. Reagan replied by outlining Watt's plan to repair roads, bridges, and trails in existing parks.[15] After the meeting, Adams told a reporter that Reagan and Watt were men who "know the cost of everything and the value of nothing."[16]

At eighty-one years of age, Adams had the courage to stand up to a president, but his health and his strength were fading. He had had a heart bypass operation in 1979, and in 1982 doctors installed an electronic pacemaker to help regulate his heartbeat. On Friday, April 20, 1984, Adams was hospitalized, complaining of pressure in his chest and shortness of breath. After a minor heart attack on Saturday, he was placed in the intensive care unit. Friends visited him on Sunday evening. Not long after they left, Adams slipped into a coma and died.

News of Adams's death was featured on every television network the next day, but despite the national interest, his family decided on a private memorial service. His body was cremated, and Michael Adams placed his father's ashes on a mountaintop in the Sierra Nevada.[17]

It is the combination of photography and the natural world that defines Ansel Adams. In photography, he was both an artist and an advocate. Adams described his first photographs, taken with a Kodak

Brownie camera, as only a "visual diary."[18] Through his hard work and his insistence on work of the highest quality, Adams established himself as a master of black-and-white photography. In addition, working with Stieglitz, Weston, Strand, Cunningham, Newhall, and others, he raised photography to a worldwide art form.

Adams was also an advocate in the world of nature. He worked to preserve wilderness areas so that the wonders that appeared in his photographs would be available for future generations. His spirit is remembered today in the Sierra Nevada he loved so much. Mount Ansel Adams stands guard along the eastern border of Yosemite National Park, and the 229,000 acres of the Ansel Adams Wilderness Area stand arm in arm with Yosemite and the John Muir Wilderness Area.

Perhaps President Jimmy Carter summed up Adams's life best in 1980. Presenting Adams with the Presidential Medal of Freedom, Carter commended the photographer for his "visionary efforts to preserve this country's wild and scenic areas both on film and on Earth."[19]

1902—Born in San Francisco, February 20.

1906—San Francisco earthquake; falls and breaks his nose.

1916—First visit to Yosemite; takes his first photographs using a Kodak Brownie camera.

1926—With encouragement from Albert Bender, begins work on his first portfolio of photographs.

1927—Photographs *Monolith, The Face of Half Dome*, in Yosemite National Park, using his technique of visualization for the first time.

1928—Marries Virginia Best; first Sierra Club outing as official photographer.

1929—Collaborates with Mary Austin to produce *Taos Pueblo*.

1930—Builds home in San Francisco; meets Paul Strand in Taos, New Mexico; chooses photography as his life's work after seeing Strand's negatives.

1931—First solo exhibition: *Pictorial Photographs of the Sierra Nevada by Ansel Adams* at the Smithsonian Institution, Washington, D.C.

1932—Group f/64 is formed.

1933—Travels to New York City and meets Alfred Stieglitz; first child, Michael, is born; holds first exhibit in New York City.

1934—Elected to board of directors of the Sierra Club.

1935—Publishes *Making a Photograph*; daughter Anne is born.

1936—Shows at Kuh Gallery in Chicago and at An American Place in New York City; lobbies in Washington, D.C., for Kings Canyon National Park using his photos.

1937—Fire in Adams's darkroom destroys about five thousand negatives.

1938—Publication of *Sierra Nevada: The John Muir Trail.*

1940—Establishes photography department with Beaumont Newhall and David McAlpin at the Museum of Modern Art (MoMA) in New York City.

1941—Accepts commission from Harold Ickes to do Mural Project—photographs of the national parks.

1943—Photographs Japanese-American internees at
–1944 Manzanar War Relocation Camp; exhibits Manzanar photos, *Born Free and Equal*, at MoMA.

1946—Receives Guggenheim Fellowship to photograph the national parks.

1948—Guggenheim Fellowship is renewed; publishes
–1949 *Yosemite and the Sierra Nevada*; begins publishing series of books on photography with *Camera* and *Lens*.

1953—Photographs "Three Mormon Towns" with Dorothea Lange.

1955—Mural photograph included in Edward Steichen's *Family of Man* exhibition at MoMA; collaborates with Nancy Newhall on *This Is the American Earth* exhibition at LeConte Memorial Lodge.

1959—Receives his third Guggenheim Fellowship to make prints of existing negatives.

1962—Moves to Carmel, California.

1963 —With Sierra Club, opposes dams threatening
–1967 Grand Canyon.

1971—Resigns from the Sierra Club board of directors after serving for thirty-seven years.

1974—Comprehensive exhibition at the Metropolitan Museum of Art.

1975—Announces he will no longer accept print orders after December 31, 1975.

1979—*Ansel Adams and the West* exhibition at MoMA.

1984—Dies on April 22 in Carmel, California.

Chapter Notes

Chapter 1. A Photograph at Dawn

1. Ansel Adams, *Ansel Adams: An Autobiography* (Boston: Little, Brown and Company, 1996), p. 221.

2. Nancy Newhall, "The Enduring Moment" (unpublished manuscript), p. 191, cited in Mary Street Alinder, *Ansel Adams: A Biography* (New York: Henry Holt and Company, 1996), pp. 202–203.

3. Ansel Adams, *Examples: The Making of 40 Photographs* (Boston: Little, Brown and Company, 1983), p. 164.

4. Jonathan Spaulding, *Ansel Adams and the American Landscape: A Biography* (Berkeley: University of California Press, 1995), p. 206.

5. Adams, *Examples,* p. 164.

6. Ibid.

7. Mary Street Alinder, *Ansel Adams: A Biography* (New York: Henry Holt and Company, 1996), p. 238.

Chapter 2. The Early Years

1. Robert Hughes, "Master of the Yosemite," *Time,* September 3, 1979, p. 42.

2. Ibid.

3. Nancy Newhall, *Ansel Adams, The Eloquent Light* (San Francisco: The Sierra Club, 1963), p. 28.

4. Ansel Adams, *Ansel Adams: An Autobiography* (Boston: Little, Brown and Company, 1996), p. 41.

5. Ibid., p. 42.

6. Ansel Adams, "Introduction," in John Muir, *Yosemite and the High Sierra,* 1948. Quoted in Nancy Newhall, *Ansel Adams, The Eloquent Light* (San Francisco: The Sierra Club, 1963), p. 29.

7. Mary Street Alinder, *Ansel Adams: A Biography* (New York: Henry Holt and Company, 1996), p. 23.

Chapter 3. The Artist as a Young Man

1. Jonathan Spaulding, *Ansel Adams and the American Landscape: A Biography* (Berkeley: University of California Press, 1995), p. 53.

2. Michael P. Cohen, *The History of the Sierra Club, 1892 to 1970* (San Francisco: Sierra Club Books, 1988), pp. 20–21.

3. Ansel Adams, *Ansel Adams: An Autobiography* (Boston: Little, Brown and Company, 1996), p. 80.

4. Mary Street Alinder and Andrea Gray Stillman, eds., *Ansel Adams: Letters and Images, 1916–1984* (Boston: Little, Brown and Company, 2001), pp. 19–20.

5. Ibid., pp. 17–18.

Chapter 4. A Short History of Photography

1. Beaumont Newhall, *The History of Photography* (New York: Museum of Modern Art, 1964), p. 19.

2. William Welling, *Photography in America, The Formative Years, 1839–1900* (New York: Thomas Y. Crowell Company, 1978), pp. 9, 21.

3. Ronald P. Lovell, Fred C. Zwahlen, Jr., James A. Folts, *Two Centuries of Shadow Catchers: A History of Photography* (New York: Delmar Publishers, Inc., 1996), p. 9.

4. Brian Coe, *The Birth of Photography* (New York: Taplinger Publishing Company, 1977), p. 53.

5. Lovell, et al., p. 167.

Chapter 5. "Let's Do a Portfolio"

1. Ansel Adams, *Ansel Adams: An Autobiography,* (Boston: Little, Brown and Company, 1996), p. 65.

2. Nancy Newhall, *Ansel Adams, The Eloquent Light* (San Francisco: The Sierra Club, 1963), p. 47.

Los Angeles Public Library
Westwood Branch
6/2/2014 5:49:09 PM

- PATRON RECEIPT -
- CHARGES -

1: Item Number: 37244153947925
  Title: Ansel Adams : America's
  Due Date: 6/23/2014

2: Item Number: 37244202620788
  Title: Ansel Adams at 100 /
  Due Date: 6/23/2014

3: Item Number: 37244158439373
  Title: Ansel Adams : American a
  Due Date: 6/23/2014

To Renew: www.lapl.org or 888-577-5275

------- Please Keep this Slip -------

3. Jonathan Spaulding, *Ansel Adams and the American Landscape: A Biography* (Berkeley: University of California Press, 1995), p. 85.

4. Adams, p. 55.

5. Ansel Adams, *Examples: The Making of 40 Photographs* (Boston: Little, Brown and Company, 1983), pp. 3–4.

6. Adams, *Autobiography*, p. 60.

7. Adams, *Examples*, p. 177.

8. Newhall, p. 79.

Chapter 6. The Making of a Photographer

1. Jonathan Spaulding, *Ansel Adams and the American Landscape: A Biography* (Berkeley: University of California Press, 1995), p. 74.

2. Ibid., p. 82.

3. Ibid., pp. 81–82.

4. Mary Street Alinder, *Ansel Adams: A Biography* (New York: Henry Holt and Company, 1996), p. 65.

5. Ibid., p. 130.

6. Ansel Adams, *Ansel Adams: An Autobiography* (Boston: Little, Brown and Company, 1996), p. 87.

7. Sue Davidson Lowe, *Stieglitz: A Memoir/ Biography* (New York: Farrar, Straus and Giroux, 1983), pp. 303, 430–435.

8. Nancy Newhall, *Ansel Adams, The Eloquent Light* (San Francisco: The Sierra Club, 1963), p. 60.

9. Nancy Newhall, *From Adams to Stieglitz: Pioneers of Modern Photography* (New York: Aperture, Inc., 1989), p. 71.

10. Lowe, p. 300.

11. Adams, pp. 87–88.

12. Alinder, p. 80.

13. Newhall, *Ansel Adams*, p. 80.

Chapter 7. Home and Away

1. Nancy Newhall, *Ansel Adams, The Eloquent Light* (San Francisco: The Sierra Club, 1963), p. 85.

2. Howard Devree, *The New York Times*, November 19, 1933, p. 12X.

3. Jonathan Spaulding, *Ansel Adams and the American Landscape: A Biography* (Berkeley: University of California Press, 1995), p. 139.

4. Mary Street Alinder and Andrea Gray Stillman, eds., *Ansel Adams: Letters 1916–1984* (Boston: Little, Brown and Company, 2001), p. 86.

5. Sam Hunter, *The Museum of Modern Art, New York: The History and the Collection* (New York: Harry N. Abrams, Inc., 1984; revised 1997), p. 18.

6. Newhall, p. 131.

7. Hunter, p. 18.

8. Newhall, p. 136.

9. Nancy Newhall, *From Adams to Stieglitz: Pioneers of Modern Photography* (New York: Aperture, Inc., 1989), p. 83.

10. Alinder and Stillman, p. 115.

Chapter 8. In the Shadow of War

1. Sam Hunter, *The Museum of Modern Art, New York: The History and the Collection* (New York: Harry N. Abrams, Inc., 1984; revised 1997), p. 24.

2. Jonathan Spaulding, *Ansel Adams and the American Landscape: A Biography* (Berkeley: University of California Press, 1995), p. 180.

3. Benita Eisler, *O'Keeffe & Stieglitz: An American Romance* (New York: Doubleday, 1991), p. 409; and Vicki Goldberg, *Margaret Bourke-White* (New York: Harper & Row, 1986), p. 152.

4. Peter Wright and John Armor, *The Mural Project: Photography by Ansel Adams* (Santa Barbara: Reverie Press, 1989), p. v.

5. Mary Street Alinder, *Ansel Adams: A Biography* (New York: Henry Holt and Company, 1996), pp. 187–188.

6. Wright and Armor, p. vi.

7. Ibid.

8. Ibid.

Chapter 9. The Apple Orchard

1. Interview with Ansel Adams in Elizabeth Partridge, ed., *Dorothea Lange: A Visual Life* (Washington: Smithsonian Institution Press, 1994), p. 157.

2. Maisie and Richard Conrat, photographs by Dorothea Lange, et al., *Executive Order 9066: The Internment of 110,000 Japanese Americans* (Los Angeles: California Historical Society, 1972), p. 5.

3. Armor and Wright, p. 4.

4. Caleb Foote, *Outcasts! The Story of America's Treatment of Her Japanese-American Minority* (New York: Fellowship of Reconciliation, 1944), p. 6.

5. Jeanne Wakatsuki Houston and James D. Houston, *Farewell to Manzanar* (Boston: Houghton Mifflin Company, 1973), pp. 65–66.

6. Ansel Adams, *Ansel Adams: An Autobiography* (Boston: Little, Brown and Company, 1985), p. 260. "Macro" was corrected to "micro" on page 220 of the paperback edition (1996).

7. Ibid.

8. Ansel Adams, *Born Free and Equal: Photographs of the Loyal Japanese Americans at the Manzanar Relocation Center, Inyo County, California* (New York: U.S. Camera, 1944), p. 5.

9. Jonathan Spaulding, *Ansel Adams and the American Landscape: A Biography* (Berkeley: University of California Press, 1995), pp. 208–209.

10. Adams, *Born Free and Equal*, p. 9.

11. David L. Jacobs, "Three Mormon Towns" *Exposure,* Vol. 25, No. 2, Summer 1987 (San Francisco: Society for Photographic Education), p. 10.

12. Armor and Wright, p. 156.

Chapter 10. A Photographer at Work

1. Ansel Adams, *Ansel Adams: An Autobiography* (Boston: Little, Brown and Company, 1996), p. 174.

2. Jonathan Spaulding, *Ansel Adams and the American Landscape: A Biography* (Berkeley: University of California Press, 1995), p. 221.

3. Mary Street Alinder and Andrea Gray Stillman, eds., *Ansel Adams: Letters and Images, 1916–1984* (Boston: Little, Brown and Company, 2001), p. 177.

4. Spaulding, p. 227.

5. Mary Street Alinder, *Ansel Adams: A Biography* (New York: Henry Holt and Company, 1996), pp. 213–214.

6. Ansel Adams with Robert Baker, *The Camera* (New York: Little, Brown and Company, 1980), p. 29.

7. Adams, *Ansel Adams,* p. 133.

8. Ansel Adams, *The Portfolios of Ansel Adams* (Boston: Little, Brown and Company, 1977, 1981), preface to Portfolio I.

9. Alinder, *Ansel Adams,* p. 222.

10. Elizabeth Partridge, ed., *Dorothea Lange, A Visual Life* (Washington: Smithsonian Institution Press, 1994), p. 157.

11. David L. Jacobs, *Exposure,* Vol. 25, No. 2, Summer 1987 (San Francisco: Society for Photographic Education), pp. 5–6.

12. Ibid., pp. 11–12.

13. Ansel Adams and Dorothea Lange, "Three Mormon Towns," *Life,* September 6, 1954, pp. 92–93.

14. Jacobs, p. 11.

15. Adams, *Ansel Adams,* p. 177.

16. Edward Steichen, "The FSA Photographers" in Beaumont Newhall, ed., *Photography: Essays & Images*, p. 267. (Reprinted from U.S. Camera, 1939, pp. 43–45.)

17. *The Family of Man* (New York: The Museum of Modern Art, 1955), p. 5.

18. Robert Hughes, "Master of the Yosemite," *Time*, September 3, 1979, p. 37.

Chapter 11. "Remember Tenaya!!!"

1. Michael P. Cohen, *The History of the Sierra Club, 1892 to 1970* (San Francisco: Sierra Club Books, 1988), pp. 20–21.

2. Jonathan Spaulding, *Ansel Adams and the American Landscape: A Biography* (Berkeley: University of California Press, 1995), p. 53.

3. Ansel Adams, *Ansel Adams: An Autobiography* (Boston: Little, Brown and Company, 1996), p. 127.

4. Cohen, p. 142.

5. Andrea Stillman and William A. Turnage, ed. *Ansel Adams: Our National Parks* (Boston: Little, Brown and Company, 1992), p. 65. (A copy of the full telegram.)

6. David Brower, *For Earth's Sake* (Salt Lake City: Peregrine Smith Books, 1990), p. 192.

7. Nancy Newhall, *Ansel Adams, The Eloquent Light* (San Francisco: The Sierra Club, 1963), p. 7.

8. Cohen, pp. 343–344.

9. Ibid., p. 363.

10. Jonathan Spaulding, *Ansel Adams and the American Landscape: A Biography* (Berkeley: University of California Press, 1995), p. 340.

11. Mary Street Alinder, *Ansel Adams: A Biography* (New York: Henry Holt and Company, 1996), p. 291.

12. Adams, p. 126.

Chapter 12. Artist Triumphant

1. Robert Hughes, "Master of the Yosemite," *Time*, September 3, 1979, p. 44.

2. Mary Street Alinder, *Ansel Adams: A Biography* (New York: Henry Holt and Company, 1996), p. 306.

3. Hilton Kramer, "Ansel Adams: Trophies from Eden," *The New York Times*, May 12, 1974, p. D23.

4. Gene Thornton, "Photography: Avedon's Father, Adams' Nature, Siskind's Homage," *The New York Times*, May 12, 1974, p. D29.

5. Alinder, p. 304.

6. Ibid., pp. 319–320.

7. Hughes, p. 36.

8. Ibid., pp. 36–37.

9. Ibid., p. 44.

10. Ansel Adams, *Ansel Adams: An Autobiography* (Boston: Little, Brown and Company, 1996), pp. 257–258.

11. Ibid., p. 296.

12. Victoria and David Sheff, "Playboy Interview: Ansel Adams," *Playboy*, May 1983, p. 82.

13. Sheff, p. 73.

14. Ibid., p. 86.

15. Dale Russakoff, "The Critique: Ansel Adams Takes Environmental Challenge to Reagan," *The Washington Post*, July 3, 1983, p. A3.

16. Ibid.

17. Alinder, pp. 371, 391.

18. Adams, p. 55.

19. Burt A. Folkart, "Ansel Adams, Artist with a Camera, Dies," *Los Angeles Times*, April 24, 1984, p. 22.

Further Reading

Adams, Ansel. *Examples: The Making of 40 Photographs.* Boston: Little, Brown and Company, 1983.

———. *The Portfolios of Ansel Adams.* Boston: Little, Brown and Company, 1977.

Adams, Ansel, John Hersey, John Armor and Peter Wright. *Manzanar.* New York: Times Books, 1988.

Cahn, Robert, and Robert Glenn Ketchum. *American Photographers and the National Parks.* New York: The Viking Press, 1981. (Includes photographs by Ansel Adams, William Henry Jackson, Timothy O'Sullivan, Edward Weston, and others.)

Dunlap, Julie, with illustrations by Kerry Maguire. *Eye on the Wild: A Story about Ansel Adams.* Minneapolis: Carolrhoda Books, Inc., 1995.

Gaines, Ann Graham. *American Photographers: Capturing the Image.* Berkeley Heights, N.J.: Enslow Publishers, Inc., 2002.

Holland, Gini. *Inventors and Inventions: Photography.* Tarrytown, New York: Benchmark Books, 1996.

Newhall, Nancy. *Ansel Adams, The Eloquent Light.* San Francisco: The Sierra Club, 1963. Reprinted: New York: Aperture, Inc., 1980. (The 1963 edition contains possibly the best reproductions of Adams's photographs in a mass-market book.)

Steichen, Edward. *The Family of Man: The Greatest Photographic Exhibition of All Time.* New York: The Museum of Modern Art, 1955. (No text: The 503 photographs speak for themselves.)

Wallace, Joseph. *Turning Points: The Camera.* New York: Atheneum Books for Young Readers, 2000.

Wright, Peter, John Armor, and Ansel Adams (photographer). *The Mural Project: Photography by Ansel Adams.* Santa Barbara: Reverie Press, 1989.

Video recording

Gray, Andrea, producer. *Ansel Adams, Photographer.* Los Angeles: Pacific Arts Video, 1991. (Includes Adams visiting with Georgia O'Keeffe.)

<http://www.anseladams.com>
The official Web site of the Ansel Adams Gallery (formerly Best's Studio) founded by Virginia Adams's father, Harry Best.

<http://www.nara.gov/nara/searchnail.html>
The National Archives and Records Administration has Adams's photos of national parks and Lange's Manzanar images.

<http://lcweb.loc.gov/rr/print/catalog.html>
The Prints and Photographs division of the Library of Congress houses photos by Dorothea Lange as well as Civil War photos, daguerreotypes, and the Farm Security Administration collection.

<http://photo.ucr.edu/photographers/adams>
The Museum of Photography at the University of California, Riverside. The Fiat Lux ("Let There Be Light") collection contains hundreds of photographs of the University of California that Adams took in the 1960s. This was for a commercial assignment honoring the university's hundredth anniversary.

<http://sunsite.berkeley.edu/calheritage>
This site sponsored by Bancroft Library at the University of California, Berkeley, includes photos of Ansel Adams; Yosemite Valley before 1890; San Francisco earthquake of 1906; Panama-Pacific Exposition of 1915; and Japanese-American relocation during World War II.

Index

Page numbers for photographs are in **boldface** type.